THE MEANING OF LIFE IN HINDUISM AND BUDDHISM

THE MEANING OF LIFE IN HINDUISM AND BUDDHISM

by

FLOYD H. ROSS

THE BEACON PRESS

BOSTON

First published 1952 by
Routledge & Kegan Paul Ltd., London
Published in U.S.A., 1953, by
The Beacon Press, Boston
Printed in Great Britain
by T. and A. Constable Ltd.
Edinburgh

TO F.J.R. AND J.F.R.

PREFACE

'The West has a good deal to learn from the East. . . . Almost every religious revival comes from the fusion of two traditions, as the Christian Church itself was, in Clement's metaphor, the confluence of two rivers, the Hellenistic and the Jewish.'—W. R. Inge.

What is the meaning of life?

How much sense of meaning does the average, thoughtful Western person have today as he looks out upon his own community and then upon the world?

How can modern man discover a meaningful sense of direction before it is too late?

These are some of the questions which Occidental man faces. What some are hailing as the dawn of a new day for the Orient can become the twilight of an old day for the Occident. Western man must open his eyes in order to experience a spiritual renaissance or he will play an increasingly maladroit role in the world community that is struggling to be born.

In a previous volume, *Addressed to Christians: Isolationism vs. World Community*, the writer discussed critically the Christian concept of 'special chosenness'. This conviction of being the 'chosen people' has led many Christians to engage in practices and to inculcate attitudes which have emphasized exclusiveness. The tragic exclusion from the Christian fellowship of many of the keenest minds and spirits of Christendom is a story that some would prefer to pass over in silence.

There is another aspect to the 'rightness and tightness' of Christian orthodoxy in practice which has been equally costly to Christendom. *No sustained attempts have been made by*

Christian leaders to arrive at sympathetic understanding of the great religious traditions of the Orient. Christendom by and large has locked itself up in its own household and has sought to live by the Graeco-Roman tradition alone. The Very Reverend W. R. Inge has well said: 'It is a reproach to us that with our unique opportunities of entering into sympathetic relations with Indian thought, we have made few attempts to do so. . . . I am not suggesting that we should become Buddhists or Hindus, but I believe that we have almost as much to learn from them as they from us.' [1]

The Christian churches have sent out missionaries to many distant lands and peoples. The 'Far East' has undoubtedly gained in many ways through this contact, but not always in the ways suspected by the missionary groups. In many cases the Eastern peoples contacted were quickened to look deeper into their own heritages. Only a few actually changed their basic religious loyalties. But the patience of the Orient in receiving the emissaries from Christendom has not helped the peoples of the West to come to a realization of their own smugness, parochialism and spiritual shallowness.

Of recent years the East has become more articulate as it has watched the symptoms of a complete breakdown in the European civilization, accented by a protracted series of wars. Thoughtful men like Ananda K. Coomaraswamy have stepped forward to protest the 'proselytizing fury' of the Occident.[2] As the chairman of Lebanon's delegation to the United Nations General Assembly has said: 'Asia is on the threshold of a great dawn, one characterized at once by an

[1] W. R. Inge, *Mysticism in Religion* (Senior Series, Hutchinson's University Library, London, n.d.), p. 8.

[2] Cf. his *Am I My Brother's Keeper?* (John Day, N.Y., 1947). Other men who have sought to mediate between the East and the West at the more profound level are Rene Guenon, Gerald Heard, Aldous Huxley, Alan Watts, Marco Pallis, D. T. Suzuki.

awakening and a revolt: the awakening is to Asia's own actualities and possibilities, the revolt is against the West, at whose hands Asia has known such humiliation, division and exploitation.'[1]

Christians must recognize the tremendous surge of the life of the spirit in the Orient, even when that surge is careless of traditional Western forms or phrases. Two tasks need to be undertaken simultaneously—the appreciative study of the Oriental traditions *at their best*, and a much more profound study of the ignored depths of Christianity at its best. If God be God of all mankind, even groups using widely differing idioms may discover they are grappling with the same problems of ultimate meanings or values. Perhaps one reason why the persons called 'Quakers' are often much more aware of the inwardness of the spiritual life is that they have less to defend in the way of outward Christian forms. The present writer must confess that he has learned more from contacts with the Society of Friends than from any other single group.

The following chapters attempt to present some of the more significant insights of Hinduism and Buddhism to Western readers. Hence this is no tourist view. The bizarre and the exotic may make good material for the picture magazines; they do not reveal much of the inner workings of the spirit of man. The fundamental question tackled by Hinduism and Buddhism is, *Who Am I?* This is a question which is receiving increased attention in psychological and religious circles in the West. Along this route modern man may come to a rediscovery of himself.

A word of appreciation to two great teachers remains to be added. Dr. J. Frank Reed of Wolverton Village, Ontario,

[1] Charles Malik, 'America and the World Crisis,' *New Outlook*, Jan. 1951, vol. 4, no. 1, p. 14.

opened many doors to an understanding of the convictions held by men standing outside the Occidental-Christian orbit. As a teacher of comparative religion in a Christian seminary, he combined scholarship, fair-mindedness and a concern for truth all too scarce in some religious circles. If Christians are to become a constructive force along with non-Christians making for what Professor Hocking has called world loyalty, it will be in part because men of the spirit and calibre of Reed refused to equate the religious quest with sectarian apologetic. Dr. Robert J. Taylor, formerly Dean of the School of Religion in the University of Southern California, stands in this same tradition.

To my wife, Frances Jenny Ross, goes a large share of the credit for making the present chapters a reality. She went through all of the preparatory drafts of the manuscript and assisted in clarifying many points. She played a secondary role of importance in protecting the study from too frequent invasion by David and Bruce. All those who combine the householder stage with the student phase of life can appreciate what is involved in this.

G. Ray Jordan, Jr., graduate student in comparative religion, offered extensive assistance both in bibliography and in criticism. To Dr. Teresina Rowell Havens, Dean Earl Cranston of the School of Religion, Alan Watts and Swami Prabhavananda, thanks are due for the valuable suggestions which came from their thoughtful scrutiny of the chapters.

F. H. ROSS.

School of Religion
University of Southern California

CONTENTS

CHAPTER ONE

THE PERENNIAL PILGRIMAGE

'He who begins by loving Christianity better than truth will proceed by loving his own sect or church better than Christianity, and end in loving himself better than all.'—S. T. COLERIDGE.

WANTED: EXPLORATORY RELIGION

RELIGION has had its name forged to so many bad checks that its premises and promises no longer carry weight with great numbers of people. The ability of the Victorian to stand inside the cloistered walls of the traditional forms of Christianity is not present in many of his grandchildren. The feeling of being at home in the tradition is denied them. Most people would probably be unable to explain just why they feel the way they do. Some try the cults, others look to Rome, still others look to Moscow. Many admit their lack of faith in all human institutions and try to accept their situation more or less philosophically.

Modern man stands on the threshold; the shape of things to come is unclear. When old faiths have died, new faiths have always appeared. Yet it is impossible ahead of time to predict in what form the new convictions will be articulated. Man's total organism is so built, however, that it never accepts a state of deprivation or disequilibrium any longer than it has to. It leans toward the future just as a tree naturally reaches up toward the sun. Unlike the tree, man tries to formulate some comprehensive theory that will help him interpret to himself what is happening. The present is all he knows or has. But to get beyond a 'little patch of immediacies', man must find some general principles in whose terms he may interpret his present.

Until recently Christianity fulfilled the role of supplying the general frame of reference for man's present tasks. Of recent decades it has increasingly failed in that function for European man and his American descendants. In part that failure is traceable to the tendency of the Christian churches to look too exclusively to the past. What happened 'once for all' could hardly happen again. Personal loyalty to *interpretations* of the founder propounded by men who lived long ago militated against loyalty to the universal insights which the founder sought to reveal.

Another reason for the decline of the influence of Christianity in Europe is that the church prided itself on its 'splendid isolation' from the great religious currents of the Orient. It insisted on drawing water only from its own well, refusing to recognize that water under other labels might be equally refreshing to the thirsty man. Whitehead has pointedly stated in his *Religion in the Making*, 'The decay of Christianity and Buddhism, as determinative influences in modern thought, is partly due to the fact that each religion has unduly sheltered itself from the other. The self-sufficient pedantry of learning and the confidence of ignorant zealots have combined to shut up each religion in its own forms of thought. Instead of looking to each other for deeper meanings, they have remained self-satisfied and unfertilized.' [1]

What is needed is a change of attitude all down the line,

[1] A. N. Whitehead, *Religion in the Making* (Macmillan, N.Y., 1926), p. 146.

not just among a few Buddhists and a handful of Christian scholars. If medieval Christianity could find it possible to assimilate most of Aristotle to itself, modern Christianity—if it has any essential vitality—can surely assimilate Gautama Buddha and other non-Christian sages. The peoples of both China and India have already shown a greater receptiveness to the suggestive insights of the West than Christendom has to the teachings of the East. If Christianity is to become a genuine vehicle for helping persons realize their vocations, it must be as ready to assimilate values from all sources as from its Palestinian and Greek past. If truth be truth, it is not tied exclusively to the soil of Judea and Attica.

Albertus Magnus and Thomas Aquinas applied themselves to the study of Greek philosophy in the thirteenth century when they noticed how many of the best young minds of Europe were being won over to the Moslem educational centres where Aristotle was an object of study. Albertus and Thomas desired to hold these students for Christendom. They went 'modernist' with a vengeance and consequently brought new life into the Christian body. They are not to be blamed for the fact that what for them was a tremendously exploratory impulse with indefinite possibilities for expansion, was subsequently frozen by churchly decree into a yardstick for doctrine.

At least since the time of Paul there has been a tendency in the Christian tradition to define the true Christian in terms of *what he believed* rather than in terms of *how* he explored. In an epistle to the Thessalonians, Paul wrote of the retribution which would be forthcoming in the last days (which he himself believed to be near) when Jesus would appear from heaven and 'in flaming fire take vengeance on them that know not God and that obey not the gospel of our Lord Jesus Christ, who shall be punished with everlasting destruction.'[1] Such language as this, emphasizing the fear of God more than the love of God, always lay near at hand for those Christians who regarded themselves as definers of orthodoxy. Yet the genius of Christianity at its best has not been in defining the faith or defending the faith but in living the faith by faith. That is the challenge which confronts it today when Christendom is suffering loss of face and of followers on a much wider scale than in the time of Thomas Aquinas.

Some from within the Christian fold may object that such a change is much too radical: Christianity can never make it and survive! That is one possible contingency. Another one—equally probable—is that if Christianity does *not* make the change, it will not survive. Even to talk about the survival of a religion, as though that were the end-all of living, is to cherish the means more than the end. It is to put religion ahead of truth or living persons; it is to claim that a vehicle is more important than the destination to which the vehicle is supposed to be conveying man. Just in this fashion religion always tends to become an idol. It is an ecclesiastically approved way of 'taking the name of the Lord in vain'.

Change is the basic fact in all of life. It was true for thousands of years before the coming of Buddha or Christ. There is no evidence to indicate that it is any less true now. Man has ever had to adapt himself as resourcefully as possible to the conditions about him. Surrounded by water, he became a fisher living primarily on the food of the sea. Surrounded by luxuriant tropical growth, he became a fruit gatherer.

[1] 2 Thessalonians i. 8-9.

Surrounded by ice, he built houses of ice blocks and lived off the polar fauna.

Throughout all the changes, man has struggled not only with hostile fellowmen but with himself. He has tried to understand himself as a part of a mysterious and frequently terrifying world. Modern man no longer believes in the objective existence of the demoniac powers and forces that troubled earlier men. Yet the demoniac powers, the divisive tendencies, have taken up their residence as neurotic compulsions within the organism. Man must come to terms with these various powers or needs, objectifying them and learning how to accept them as part of the total human picture. The old religious symbols are no longer adequate. Their very definiteness for earlier generations makes them most inadequate for today. Modern man's problem must be redefined in the light of the dynamics of the inner life, not in terms of beings residing 'out there'. Spalding has commented that in the religion of the Semites and the Latins everything is 'as vivid, as sharply defined, as the objects around them, clear-cut in the light of the sub-tropical sun: God and Devil, Heaven and Hell, angels and demons, saints and damned'.[1] That very definiteness must now be sacrificed if man is to take substantial strides in gaining a sense of orientation.

This is not particularly different from what has, to some degree, always been the case. All of the eminent religious teachers have said in one way or another that while many may consider themselves called, few are actually chosen. Of the many who have followed the pathway of traditional religious practices, only a few have found true centredness.

[1] H. N. Spalding, *Civilization in East and West* (Oxford, London, 1939), p. 147.

The risks have always been there; the razor's edge has not been easy to find.

RELIGIONS—A MIXED GOOD

All religions are a mixed good. They reflect the ambiguities of the human situation in whatever culture they are found. Sometimes religions appear to have been the main instrument of cultural development; at other times they have been obstacles to man's larger fulfilment. Religion which expresses life creatively never binds man to itself. Religion which compensates for life binds man to itself by demanding unswerving orthodoxy, strict obedience, rigid conformity. Man then becomes compulsively religious.

In the history of religion, men can be found worshipping their tribal gods in wholehearted ways. They can be seen cowering before their gods in abject fear and insecurity. They can be seen praying to their own wants but with the names of deities upon their lips: 'Give us victory in battle. . . . Give us sons. . . . Give us raiment.' They can be seen accepting the universe around them with dignity and joy. Some men walk upright, others prostrate themselves before an idol made of wood or words. Whether the gods be thought of as one or many, the fundamental attitudes remain essentially the same.

The history of religion is thus not necessarily a record of progress. Inner progress in the mind of the honest explorer is difficult to measure. Outer progress is debatable. God concepts and systems of thought proliferate like weeds. Sometimes it is hard to know which is a weed and which a flower. In every religious tradition there is someone cast in the role of the priest, seeking to persuade his flock that the tribal religion offers the answer to every problem. The priest who is 'set apart' is always an interested party; his words must be weighed. At times more wisdom is found on the lips of the anti-clerical than on the altar of the priest. The Pharisee or the Puritan may be an honourable man, but his critics must also be heard.

Histories of the living religions have been written both by friends of specific traditions and by religion's cultured despisers. In such cases the point which was to be proved frequently illuminated only a small portion of the human scene. When history is written only for the orthodox, items which will not serve as props to a specific faith are usually screened out. The end result is to 'confirm' those already in the faith and to strengthen their feelings of superiority. If the history is written only for the cultured despisers, the same process is involved negatively—any constructive features of religion will be toned down or omitted.

It should be possible to study the religions of the world without trying to prove either the superiority of religion or of irreligion. If the human, psychological foundations for both religion and irreligion are closely interrelated, the important task is to inquire into the dynamics of belief (or of unbelief, if that is the object of immediate interest). Since large-scale unbelief is a relatively recent phenomenon, it would seem pertinent to inquire into the roots of religious beliefs first. The honest inquirer will take a position, not treating it like a medieval castle behind whose walls he retreats, but as a point of departure for further inquiry. Albert Schweitzer has expressed this forcibly: 'If thought is to set out on its journey unhampered, it must be prepared for anything, even for arrival at intellectual agnosticism. But even if our will-to-action is destined to wrestle endlessly and unavailingly with an agnostic view of the universe and of life, still this painful disenchantment is better for it than persistent refusal to think out its position at all. For this disenchantment does, at any rate, mean that we are clear as to what we are doing.' [1] The capacity to set out confidently in an exploratory way is one significant measure of the quality of one's faith.

The story of man's religious pilgrimage need not be written either for conformers or non-conformers. It should be directed to those who have not forgotten the joy of youth in searching, in finding, and in setting forth to search again. Only by accident does the history of religion serve to bolster the morale of any specific theological fraternity or anti-clerical cult. The proper study of mankind is man and his capacities for growth and the realization of larger values. Both the religions and the protests against them are an important part of man's coming of age. If the gods die, it is when they have no real basis in enlarging experience. If God be real, he needs no defence.

Western man has sought to live unto himself for too many centuries. He has fed on his own past almost exclusively, learning little from the Far East. His diet has proved somewhat deficient. The decay of Western civilization—most evident in Europe in recent decades—is paralleled by the decay of Christianity as a vital force. The wisdom of the East may act as a catalytic agent in the West, where people are still too inclined to regard Europe or the Mediterranean world as the sole Mt. Sinai of the human family.

If Western man is to reassess his place in history, he must venture beyond his own bailiwick. No glassy-eyed stare to-

[1] Albert Schweitzer, *Decay and Restoration of Civilization* (Black, London, 1947), p. 104.

ward the Orient will be of any value. One of the eminent schools of depth psychology in the West consciously draws upon the insights of the East.[1] This is an encouraging sign. The peoples of the Orient inquired into the conditions of human happiness centuries before the West did. Starting from within, they sought to understand the art of living. European man has often neglected this art because of his zeal for technology and manipulation of the physical environment. Now that he feels 'hag-ridden by the future', with its threat of continuing wars, Western man may be ready to attempt a more proper balance between the call of the outer world and the needs of the inner man.

POSTSCRIPT ON 'RELIGION' AND 'METAPHYSIC'

This is no place for adding to the already lengthy list of definitions of religion. However, the reader needs to be aware of the fact that such scholars on the Orient as Coomaraswamy and Guenon differentiate between Western *religion* and Oriental *metaphysic*. Religion has a great deal of what they term the sentimental factor. God is described in terms of human feelings and senses or desires and thus is portrayed in positive terms. Religion also is interested in historical factors such as 'the fulness of time', or the authenticity of certain alleged books and the historicity of eminent persons.

Metaphysic, on the other hand, is not primarily interested in establishing historical facts but in arriving at universal truths which have no necessary connection with the time-track. The factor of sentiment is nil. Where religion seeks to be positive and reassuring, metaphysic is completely dis-

[1] Cf. Carl G. Jung's Foreword to D. T. Suzuki's *An Introduction to Zen Buddhism* (Philosophical Library, N.Y., 1949), p. 26.

interested in the search for truth. To take an analogy from the space-time world, the 'law of gravity' is not designed to give comfort to anybody. It represents an effort to articulate in disinterested fashion the operation of a universal principle.

Alan Watts has put the distinction quite concisely: 'Both Vedanta and Buddhism tend to describe the ultimate Reality in terms of what it is *not*, and Christianity in terms of what it is *like*.' [1] Religion is thus quite pictorial and 'space-bound' in its attempts to describe God and immortality. It tends to 'locate' God as well as Heaven, and almost inevitably describes immortal life in terms of unending duration.

Metaphysic is much more closely related to the purest form of scientific inquiry where what is sought is the most comprehensive meaning of all. It is also related to the arts since they 're-present' the deepest intuitions of life. In metaphysic what is called for is the extension of man's area of consciousness, not the merely technological extension of his hands and brain. One does not explain music to a deaf mute, nor ask him to seek a cure through constructing finer musical instruments. Rather one seeks to cure his deafness.

W. E. Hocking has said that religion contains the release from all localism and from all historical accidents.[2] However, religion released from localism is no longer religion in the ordinary meaning of the term. It is *high* religion, or what

[1] Alan W. Watts, *The Supreme Identity* (Pantheon, N.Y., 1950), p. 59. Watts points out that this distinction was made by one of the early Christian mystics, Dionysius the Areopagite (so-called). Cf. C. E. Rolt's translation of *Dionysius on the Divine Names and the Mystical Theology* (Macmillan, N.Y., 1940), p. 200. Cf. Rene Guenon, *Introduction to the Study of the Hindu Doctrines* (Luzac, London, 1945), ch. 4, esp. pp. 103-6.

[2] W. E. Hocking, *Living Religions and a World Faith* (Macmillan, N.Y., 1940), p. 35.

Guenon means by the word metaphysic; for it has died to itself in pointing on to a transcendent meaning or reality that forever eludes definition or limitation.

Every person is a metaphysician who has not lost his capacity for native wonder or sustained and intelligent search. India developed a significant civilization long before European tribes emerged from semi-barbarism. Many of the most penetrating questions which human beings have ever faced were propounded there. To India we now turn our attention.

CHAPTER TWO

ANCIENT INDIA LOOKS AT LIFE

'They call him many who is really One.'
'Even as he seems, so he becomes.'—*Rig Veda*.

INDIA has often been described as a land of mystery. If this is so, it is partly because Occidentals have not sought sympathetically to enter into her life and thought. Not many years before the end of his life, Coomaraswamy wrote that 'it would be hardly an exaggeration to say that a faithful account of Hinduism might well be given in the form of a categorical denial of most of the statements that have been made about it, alike by European scholars and by Indians trained in our modern sceptical and evolutionary modes of thought.' [1]

What Coomaraswamy is objecting to is the tendency on the part of so many European scholars to over-emphasize the purely relative and historical aspects of comparative religion, and to assume that the latest is necessarily the most profound expression of a basic truth or intuition. The usual Western interpretation claims that monotheism arose late in the reli-

[1] A. K. Coomaraswamy, *Hinduism and Buddhism* (Philosophical Library, N.Y., 1943), p. 8. Cf. Rene Guenon, *East and West* (Luzac, London, 1941); Guenon, *Introd. to the Study of the Hindu Doctrines; Man and His Becoming According to the Vedanta* (Luzac, London, 1945); A. K. Coomaraswamy, *A New Approach to the Study of the Vedas*; Coomaraswamy, *Buddha and the Gospel of Buddhism* (Harrap, London, 1928); Coomaraswamy, *Am I My Brother's Keeper?* (John Day, N.Y., 1947); Alan W. Watts, *The Supreme Identity*; Marco Pallis, *Peaks and Lamas* (Knopf, N.Y., 1949).

gion of ancient India, growing out of an earlier polytheism. The Eastern scholar can reply that there is more so-called 'polytheism' in the late *Vedic* hymns than in the early period, a fact which hardly fits into the Western theory of progress or 'evolution'.

Gradually the distorted picture of Indian philosophy and metaphysic is being corrected. The West is coming to realize that there were great ideas and civilizations before 'the golden age of Greece'. Many are ready to admit that Guenon may not be far from the truth when he says that 'the position of the West in relation to the East is that of a branch growing out of the trunk'.[1]

That India had what is commonly termed a 'high' civilization three thousand years ago has long been known to the West. India's influence upon the West through the mediation of the Greeks and the Arabs has been the subject of many studies. More recently the archaeological discoveries at Harappa and Mohenjo-daro, in the north and north-west of India, have made it clear that there was a highly developed civilization in the Indus valley between 3000 and 2500 B.C.[2] These cities were flourishing centres of trade a thousand years before the Aryan-speaking people entered India. The people who built them were in no sense semi-barbarous. In the complete absence of any lengthy documents, it is impossible to know what their literary productions were. Enough has been learned, however, from the brief inscriptions on seals and amulets to indicate that they exerted real influence on the religious life of India centuries later.

[1] Guenon, *Introd. to the Study of the Hindu Doctrines*, p. 31.

[2] Cf. Ernest Mackay, *The Indus Civilization* (Dickson & Thompson, London, 1935), ch. 3.

THE MORE EXTERNAL VIEW OF THE RIG VEDIC RELIGION

There is a more casual view of the religion of the *Rig Vedic* period which is commonly held in the West. It can be stated very briefly for our purposes, largely to show the contrast between it and the much more provocative and profound interpretation of the Eastern scholars.

The *Rig Veda* is a collection of 1028 hymns and is regarded by Western scholars as the oldest and most important of the sources for an understanding of Indian religion. It is usually dated not earlier than 1300 B.C. From these hymns the scholars have reconstructed a picture of the people who produced them. They were apparently healthy-minded activists who invaded India from the north-west somewhere between 2500 and 1500 B.C. They migrated from an invigorating climate down through the mountain passes into the subcontinent of India. For them, as for many other peoples, India became the end of the road. In successive waves the tribes moved forward with domestic animals, agricultural implements and war equipment. They brought with them their ancient tribal myths and legends.[1]

The numerous hymns of the *Rig Veda* reveal that the invaders were hard fighters and heavy drinkers. They sought the physical goods of life with few inhibitions and uncritically accepted them as a kind of heaven-bestowed bounty. There was no marked tendency to inquire into those inner conditions that might permit the highest development of man's capacities. Sons, wealth, victory in battle, long life—these

[1] A. B. Keith, *The Religion and Philosophy of the Veda and Upanishads* (Harvard Oriental Series, vols. 31, 32, Cambridge, 1925), vol. 31, p. 1. Keith can be taken as fairly representative of Western scholarship. He expresses his indebtedness to a dozen outstanding Western scholars.

were the goods they sought. In addition they desired ample *soma*, a potent beverage made from a plant bearing that name.

The cosmic powers they believed in were a reflection of themselves in that they were mostly conceived in the form of man. Most of them also had some direct connection with natural phenomena—the earth, the atmosphere or the heavenly bodies. Their gods functioned primarily to supply man with the things he wanted. There were different levels of divine powers. The ancestral spirits were on the lowest level. On proper occasions they had to be honoured and fed. Above them were the gods of nature with their departmental duties. In the background lurked the relatively impersonal creator-gods like *Prajapati* (Lord of Creatures) and *Brahmanaspati* (Lord of Prayer).

The personalized nature-gods—*Varuna*, *Indra*, *Agni* and *Soma*—were the powers besought by the worshippers seeking specific goods. In the earliest period of the *Rig Veda*, *Varuna* seems to have been the pre-eminent god. He was regarded as the all-seeing eye and was symbolized by the sun with its countless rays. It was *Varuna* who saw into the hearts of men when they were devising some evil deed. If two men sat together in secret, *Varuna* was always present as a third. *Varuna* was regarded as the guardian of the *Rita*—the law of nature, of the ceremonial sacrifice and the moral law as well. The ethical overtones in the worship of *Varuna* were pronounced.

In the period of the conquest of India the worship of *Varuna* suffered. *Indra*, who was god of battles, bearer of the thunderbolt, and champion *soma* drinker, gained the ascendency. He was the favourite god of the warriors. *Indra* is the subject of over 250 hymns in the *Rig Veda.* There are several vivid descriptions of his appearance. He has arms, hands and a head after the fashion of ordinary men, and a belly as large as a lake. On one occasion he drinks thirty lakes full of *soma.* He usually feeds on 100 to 300 buffaloes. His greatest single deed is the slaying of a serpent lying on the mountains holding back the waters of the streams.

Agni, god of the sacred fire, was also very prominent in the religion of these invaders. In the eyes of the priesthood *Agni* was second only to *Indra.* Whereas *Indra* was thought of as delivering victory in battle, *Agni* was regarded as bearer of prosperity and happiness to the home. Closely associated with *Agni* was *Soma*, god of the potent oblation. An elaborate mythology grew up around *Soma.* He is pictured as the bull who fertilizes the waters, his cows. He is the giver of potency to men. His beverage is the elixir of immortality. When the *soma* liquid was poured out on the altar in the ritual, it was *Agni*, the chaplain of the gods, who took the oblation aloft. In later years both *Agni* and *Soma* were to become the principal objects of priestly interest.

Each household seems to have had its own priest in the earlier *Rig Vedic* period. In many cases the father must have filled this role. In the household of a tribal chieftain or king, a chaplain was appointed to take care of those important rites. The chaplain came to be known as a priest of *Brahman.* Gradually the king's chaplain acquired increasing status and a priestly caste emerged. These priests (styled 'Brahmans') tended to become the kings' advisers on many matters in addition to the performance of the ritual. The details of the many sacrifices offered to the gods were their chief concern.

TOWARD PROFESSIONALISM IN RELIGION: THE BRAHMANAS

Shortly after 1000 B.C. the religion of these Indo-Europeans who had settled down in India underwent a change. Some interpreters stress the part that climate and diet may have played in this. The climate was friendly, the land bountifully productive, so that the conqueror had more time on his hands than he could fill with his traditional activities native to cooler climates. In any event changes began to appear in the attitudes of the conquering people. Many of these changes can be sensed in the later hymns of the *Vedic* period as well as in the ritual commentaries written by the priests between 1000 and 800 B.C., known as the *Brahmanas*. These commentaries were the product of priestly speculation upon the earlier collections of hymns and chants.

The natural healthy outgoingness of the earlier period had apparently died away. In its place arose a preoccupation with the formal side of the religion, the ritual of the sacrifice. This seems to have been accompanied by a certain clouding of reflective thought. The earlier theology faded, but no dynamic or new theology arose to replace it. The clear concepts of the *Rig Vedic* gods began to become blurred and indistinct as though the gods were no longer real, but belonged to a distant country. One result of this was that the priesthood gained increasing prominence. Were not the priests the professional experts on the ceremonies? The names of the gods tended to become mere counters in the grand manipulative process of the sacrifice. Since the sacrifice was always directed to the interests of specific individuals (not as in China, where the sacrifices were for the benefit of the people collectively), different sacrifices had to be performed many more times. An elaborate sacrifice might require the services of many priests over a period of days or even months.

The principal good sought by the worshipper through the rite of the sacrifice was immortal life in some happy state beyond the grave. Other-worldly religion in the form of a postponed hedonism displaced the this-worldly religion of the *Rig Vedic* period. Both the sacrifice and the priests became indispensable. The priests who formerly had been functionaries of the old gods now became more important than the gods. Priestly religion was in the saddle, trying to supply what the masses desired.

This concern with death and its aftermath is underscored by a story in the *Satapatha Brahmana.* The gods themselves at one time feared death, the mighty 'Ender'. 'So with toilsome rites they worshipped and performed religious acts till they became immortal. Then the Ender said to the gods, "As ye have made yourselves imperishable, so will men endeavour to free themselves from me; what portion then shall I possess in man?" The gods replied, "Henceforth no being shall become immortal in his own body; this his mortal frame shalt thou still seize; this shall remain thy own. He who through knowledge or religious works henceforth attains to immortality shall first present his body, Death, to thee." '[1]

This concern about achieving a happy after-life played directly into the hands of the priests. The priesthood tended to exploit the situation at the expense of the masses. The priestly apparatus became too expensive for the common

[1] Translation by M. Monier-Williams, *Indian Wisdom* (Luzac, London, 1893).

man to hire. Only the wealthy few could take it or leave it. The more thoughtful persons began to withdraw to meditate anew upon the ancient themes.

The first attempts to escape the rigors of the costly priestly system took the form of substituting *meditation* upon the sacrifice for the sacrifice itself. The elaborate horse sacrifice normally took months to perform and a large retinue of priests. This was now cast into a subjective mould. The sacrifice was performed meditatively with the whole universe, in various aspects, being the horse, the altar and the priest. In other words, the sacrificial system was spiritualized.

Out of this interiorization process eventually came what is frequently termed in the West as the '*Upanishadic* reformation'. The literary by-products are known as the *Upanishads* and are usually dated between 800 and 600 B.C. In them the religion of the Indo-Europeans is supposed to have reached the peak of its 'development'. The Indian sages now applied themselves to the problem of immortality and promulgated the teaching on the identity of the *Atman* (the real Self in man) with *Brahman* (the Cosmic Reality). Other teachings and practices, including the various forms of *yoga*, are supposed to have developed in the centuries following the *Upanishads*.[1]

THE TRADITIONAL EASTERN VIEW

When all of the above has been said, the profounder part of the Indian position has scarcely been plumbed. Such Western terms as 'pantheism', 'nature worship' and 'poly-

[1] See chapter 4.

theism' have been thrown around freely. What is overlooked is the underlying theme of unity:

> *They call him many who is really One.*
> *Even as he seems, so he becomes.* [1]

That is, the Supreme Reality is One, but the needs of the various worshippers lead to the multiplication of names and concepts. Ancient India brought forth life bountifully; likewise the people continued to apply new-found names in great diversity to the one underlying principle. This seems to have been accompanied by a tendency on the part of many to conceive of the names as applying to independent powers or divine beings.

The seers, however, were always conscious of the One, not the many. This insight they regarded as timeless in origin, unaffected by the human need for diversity of expressions. For them *Veda* meant literally *traditional knowledge* of immemorial antiquity. When Eastern writers refer to 'the timelessness of the *Veda*', they are not referring to the literary documents upon which historical critics work. No written or spoken statement or interpretation can be definitive. *They mean the traditional wisdom which has always been available to all men of awareness at all times*. It is an inwardly appropriated wisdom which *in principle* has nothing to do with time and place. *In practice*, time, place and circumstance have very much to do in shaping the expression of the insights.

Hence, where Western scholars are inclined to talk about 'development of doctrine', Eastern students see only change in expression of the doctrine. The language of the *Vedas* is more archaic than the language of the *Upanishads*, yet the

[1] *Rig Veda* X.114.5; cf. III.5.4; V.3.1; V.44.6.

ideas of the *Upanishads* are to be found in the *Vedas*.[1] Indian scholars do not take purely documentary considerations too seriously, for back of the literary sources lies a period of oral transmission of indeterminate length. In ancient India all instruction in the more important matters was given only in face-to-face situations. This ties in with the traditional interpretation of the word '*Upanishad*' as meaning secret doctrine or mystery. The student received it personally from a sage.

For centuries Western scholars on the whole have tended to be more interested in how a doctrine comes to be articulated than in what the doctrine means. This is somewhat analogous to the child taking a clock to pieces in great joy but totally unconcerned with the meaning of time or duration.

CENTRAL AFFIRMATION OF INDIAN METAPHYSIC

What is the central affirmation of Indian metaphysic? It is *the affirmation of the supreme identity of man, in the real depths of his Selfhood, with the highest transcendental Reality*. This identity can be 'known' intuitively in the highest reaches of consciousness. Such 'knowledge' is self-authenticating, just as one 'knows' water satisfies thirst by drinking of it, not theorizing about it. Hence, in India to 'know God' does not mean that 'I' (the subject) know 'God' (the object); for the highest 'knowledge' involves the realization that subject and object are *one* in a deeper sense than any physical analogy could make clear.

This thought of unity, or of the 'knowledge' that authenticates itself in an intuitive awareness, dominates the traditional

[1] Coomaraswamy, *A New Approach to the Study of the Vedas*, p. 54. He cites *Rig Veda* VI.16.35 and V.46.1.

doctrine of India. The unity has been conceived in many different ways—mythologically, ritually, philosophically. The diversity of interpretations has completely misled Western scholars who are conditioned to regard *some* doctrine as definitive and all others as false. Christian dogmatic theology, crystallized and promulgated by the administratively successful, set the pattern in the European environment. All views out of line with the officially approved 'definition' were anathematized. The latter-day progeny of Theology, 'the Queen of the Sciences', have followed the royal administrative pattern in being equally autocratic in the secular frame of reference: often in the sciences (physical or social) a *view* is not regarded as a 'point of view' but as an exclusive dogma ruling out other ways of viewing experience.

Guenon reminds Western students of philosophy that 'the diverse metaphysical and cosmological conceptions of India are not, strictly speaking, different doctrines, but only developments of a single doctrine according to different points of view and in various, but by no means incompatible, directions.' [1] Such plurality of viewpoints is inevitable since people differ in temperament. Furthermore, whenever they look at any object—a mountain for example—they necessarily stand in different places and have different perspectives.[2]

All the points of view begin and end with the problem of unity or non-duality. As the unchanging Reality behind the universe, this unity is called *Brahman*. As the indestructible

[1] Guenon, *Man and His Becoming*, p. 14.

[2] The Sanskrit word *darshana*, 'point of view', comes from a root which means seeing. Often it has been translated as 'school'.

Spirit or Self in man, it is called *Atman*.[1] In no case is the unity to be defined in terms of this thing or that thing, this concept or that concept. One can only approach the realization of it by negating all particular experiences or ideas. It is 'not this, not this' (*neti, neti*).

This point of view is difficult for Westerners to grasp, largely because of the Occidental tendency to 'reify' and then 'deify' the highest goals, goods or concepts of individual or social experience. This is to make pseudo-absolutes out of very relative efforts, as though a child were to treat his castles in the sand as if they were real dwellings. He who has been conditioned to regard as meaningful only that which can be touched, tasted or analysed finds it hard to realize that there may be areas of reality that elude his sense-organs and his logic. Such a person may be reminded that the human ear can record only a small proportion of the vibrations that are actually presented to it; but if he is quite satisfied with what he does hear, he brushes aside as either irrelevant or non-existent that which he has not acquired the sensitivity for hearing.

Just how or when this conventionalized wall-of-non-awareness (or tone-deafness) can be breached is not predictable. Yet if the effort is honestly made, it may turn out to be rewarding. Let us turn to a condensed version of the Indian Myth regarding this unity, to see what light may be thrown upon the subject. After an examination of the Myth,

[1] *Atman*, from root *an*, to breathe, is Spirit in its primary meaning; it has taken on the secondary sense of 'self', where it can stand for the bodily self, the psychic self, or the spiritual self. Coomaraswamy translates it by 'Self' rather than Spirit, and uses a small initial letter when he is referring to the empirical (or psychophysical) self. I have followed his practice in this regard (Coomaraswamy, *Hinduism and Buddhism*, p. 34).

the *Upanishadic* analysis of the same problem will be dealt with, followed by the *Gita's* treatment of the perennial theme.

THE MYTH

As indicated earlier, the affirmation of the supreme identity of the Self (*Atman*) with ultimate Reality (*Brahman*) has been presented in a variety of ways in India. The very profuseness of the poet's mythological expressions has been one of the stumbling-blocks in the path of the Western students who have sought to understand the *Vedas*. The major obstacle, however, has been the Occidental's lack of appreciation for myth and poetry as avenues of insight. This warning must in all fairness be given to that person who approaches the Indian Myth for the first time, lest he be dismayed when he fails to catch all of the subtle nuances.[1]

The Myth deals with an eternal 'in the beginning'. It does not presume to give a 'scientific' account of the origin of species, of the Earth, or of the solar system. The validity of the Myth is not tied up with the questions of dates or 'when did it happen?' (Analogously, when a small child asks 'Who made the stars?', his question arises far more out of wonder and awe than out of a desire for a cut-and-dried answer, with blueprints and production details supplied.) The language of the Myth is thus quite incidental, for it is designed to point the wondering person on from finite or temporal data to timeless meanings or values. Hence the Myth can be told in many ways and varying idioms so long as the words used are not tied down to purely surface usages.

[1] Cf. H. Zimmer, *Myths and Symbols in Indian Art and Civilization* (Pantheon, N.Y., 1947; Thames and Hudson, London, 1950).

The first three verses of the Hymn of Creation (*Rig Veda* X.129) provide the point of departure.

Existence was not, nor its opposite,
Nor earth, nor heaven's blue vault, nor aught beyond.
The subtle elements that are the veil
Of this so insubstantial world, where then
Might they find out a place? by whom be known?
The deep abyss of waters—where was that?

Death was not yet, nor deathlessness; the day
Was night, night day, for neither day nor night
Had come to birth. Then THAT, *the primal fount*
Of light—immobile—rest and action joined—
Brooded in silent bliss. Itself beside,
In the wide universe there nothing was.

In the beginning gloom—gloom hidden in gloom!
From its cause undistinguished stood the world:
But lo, thereafter, from its darkling state
(Yet undistinguished from its cause), it rose,
By the pure will of THAT *made manifest.*[1]

In the eternal beginning there is only the supreme identity of THAT ONE, the undifferentiated 'ALL', beyond both existence and non-existence. Western thought, with its pragmatic-utilitarian bent, hesitates to go this far back in its statement of first principles. Yet even the astronomer who tries to explain the origin of this planetary system or this particular galaxy, assumes some such undifferentiated whole, even

[1] Translation by Swami Prabhavananda and F. Manchester in *Voice of India*, vol. 3, no. 1, Jan. 1940, pp. 1-2. Cf. Coomaraswamy, *A New Approach to the Study of the Veda*, pp. 54-5.

though on the physical plane exclusively. The psychologist, though he may not venture to speak about anything more than the relation between a 'psyche' and a 'soma' as in psychosomatic medicine, assumes a larger state of unity or wholeness in the person he is trying to help. Perhaps it is a certain timidity, akin to adolescent awkwardness, which restrains Western man from going back to a metaphysical unity as the starting-point for all fundamental discussion. In practically all worldly discussions of diversities, there seems to be some assumption of a prior unity—prior in the metaphysical sense though not necessarily prior in the temporal sequence.

'That One', according to the Indian Myth, is the universally Real which can 'objectify' itself in finite worlds or creatures but can never be an object of knowledge since it is no 'object' or 'no-thing'. It is the Eternal Subject or the Great Self (*Para Brahman* or *Paratman*). The finite world is made possible only when 'That One' submits to a dismemberment. This is pictured as a Sacrifice. By this passion or Sacrifice, the Supreme Self creates the world of men; by entering into their bodies and opening up the apertures of the senses and the mind, he awakens them to consciousness. As such he is the 'Eye in the World', symbolized by the sun in the outer world and by fire (*Agni*, 'inner light') in the inner world of man's heart.[1]

The Supreme Self as the 'Inner Man' has been swallowed by the 'Outer Man', by the sense of individuality or egoism. Each human being is bound to be at war with himself until he finds out *Who* he really is. Day after day the 'Outer Man'

[1] Cf. *Maitrayana Brahmana Up.* 2.6; *Taittiriya Samhita* II.9.3; II.3.8.1-2; II.5.8.2.; *Rig Veda* X.124.4; X.90.6-8; X.31.7; X.81.4; I.32.

goes on dismembering the 'Inner Man', the real Self. An expiation for this condition is provided for in the Sacrifice, specifically the Burnt-offering. This is simply a symbolic imitation of the Sacrifice 'in the beginning'. In this ritual the sacred libation of *Soma* is poured into the sacred fire as into God's mouth.[1] The person doing the sacrificing builds up again the dismembered deity through surrendering his egoism or dividedness.

Looked at in this perspective, the tenth book of the *Satapatha Brahmana* takes on real meaning for any student of depth psychology. This chapter deals in detail with the construction of the great Fire Altar. The altar represents not only the structure of the universe but also the Supreme Self, the creator and primal victim. When the sacred libation is poured into the sacred fire and the entire ceremony completed, the unity of creation is restored and the dismembered body of the Supreme Self is brought back to life.[2]

The Sacrifice is thus an eternal process, something to be 'lived through' by every person. The physical elements—the fire on the altar and the libation—are only symbols. Ignorant persons may go through the outer forms completely unaware of what they are really doing. But the *Rig Veda* makes clear that what the aware person understands by *Soma* is 'consumed in the heart'.[3]

The enlightened person is not engaging in some form of crude magic. He is making a Burnt-offering of his 'Outer Self'. In thus slaying his own 'Dragon', his illusion of separ-

[1] Coomaraswamy, *Hinduism and Buddhism*, p. 22.

[2] *Satapatha Brahmana* X.

[3] *Rig Veda* X.8.34; I.168.3; I.179.5.

ateness, he gains his rebirth. The inner war is now over for one has found his cosmic reintegration. For him who performs the outer Sacrifice 'knowing not this interior Burnt-offering, it is as if he pushed aside the brands and made oblation in the ashes'.[1] But for the illumined person, participation in the Sacrifice is not the perfect, meticulous celebration of external rites. Rather, the perfect fulfilling of one's vocation is itself the celebration of the rite.

The Western student is almost bound to interpret the Myth, at least initially, in subjective-psychological terms. This is not a bad approach so long as one remains aware of the profound cosmic implications in the Myth as viewed by the Indian. What is sought through the ritual is *Self-knowledge*. (The Sanskrit terms for this are *Atma-jnana*.) The person who becomes aware of a sense of inner alienation raises the question, 'Who am I?' From there it is a natural step to distinguish between the 'Outer Man' (which the Western psychologist is dealing with as the psychophysical self) and the 'Inner Man' (the real Self from which one feels alienated while retaining intimations of It). Each person desires autonomy or 'self-control'. Out of his sense of dividedness and his consciousness of an 'I' and a 'mine' over against a 'thou' and a 'thine', he seeks to move in the direction of a unifying consciousness. 'As one embraced by a darling bride knows naught of "I" and "thou", so self embraced by the fore-knowing (solar) Self knows naught of a "myself" within or a "thyself" without.' Or again, 'As all spokes are contained in the axle and in the felly of a wheel, all beings and all those

[1] *Sankhyana Aranyaka* X. Cf. *Satapatha Brahmana* II.2.4.7; III.8.1.2; *Taittiriya Samhita* II.5.4.5; Coomaraswamy, *Hinduism and Buddhism*, p. 23.

selves are contained in that Self.' [1] One's sense of alienation is overcome through the enlarging of one's consciousness, not through adjustment to fragmentary demands of the social or physical order.

BY WAY OF TRANSITION

So much for a condensation of the mythological statement of the Indian tradition. The following chapters will amplify portions of these in the language of the *Upanishads* and the *Bhagavad Gita*. The *Upanishads* constitute what is known as the *Vedanta* or 'end of the *Veda*'. They form the last portion of the *Vedic* texts and their teachings reflect the traditional insights in their entirety.

The *Upanishads* are concerned with knowledge of God and knowledge of Self.[2] These two reduce to one fundamental knowledge or awareness, as even a Christian writer, Meister Eckhart, has expressed it: 'No one can know God who has not first known himself. . . . Since we find God in oneness, that oneness must be in him who is to find God.' [3]

Basic to the Indian outlook on life is the desire of the individual to be identified with that which is not transient. If the reader bears this fact in mind, he will understand better some of the precise distinctions made by the *Upanishadic* sages. They distinguished, for example, between the individual ego or 'soul' (*jivatma*) and the Self (*Atman*). The former is the empirical ego of most modern psychology which can be an object of study since it is an aggregate of sensations,

[1] *Brihadaranyaka Upanishad* 4.3.21 (following Coomaraswamy's translation, which is freer than Müller's); 2.5.15.

[2] God knowledge=*Brahman-vidya*. Self knowledge=*Atman-jnana*.

[3] R. Blakney, *Meister Eckhart: A Modern Translation* (Harper, N.Y., 1941), Fragment 37; The Aristocrat, p. 80.

feelings, and so on. *The Self, however, is the knowing subject which is* never *an object.* It is pure consciousness or awareness. It is implied in all knowing but is not known.

Another fundamental distinction in terms is that between *Brahman*, the unmanifested Supreme Principle, and *Brahma*, God manifested as personal deity.[1] Indian literature uses many names and attributes to characterize *Brahma.* Yet it is recognized that behind the 'named' there is the Name-less, the living Reality which can never be conceptualized—*Brahman.* In the words of Nikhilananda: '*Brahman* does not exist as an empirical object—for instance, like a pot or a tree—but as Absolute Existence, without which material objects would not be perceived to exist. Just as a mirage cannot be seen without the desert, which is its unrelated substratum, so also the universe cannot exist without *Brahman.*' [2]

In the following pages, technical terms will be held to a minimum. Those who wish to use the more precise terms will find a Glossary at the end of the book. Where dynamic psychological concepts from Western thought have been drawn upon, one is not to infer that the traditional teachings have *only* a psychological dimension. This is untrue, for a

[1] There is no typographically convenient way of distinguishing in English between the Sanskrit neuter form and the masculine form, nor is there agreement among the scholars on the matter of transliteration. For convenience in the following treatment, the term *Brahman* is to be understood as applying to the Absolute or Supreme Principle, which can only be described negatively. *Brahma* will be used when God-as-personal is meant. When only priests of *Brahman* are referred to, the context will make it clear, thus obviating the use of a third term 'Brahmin' (cf. A. K. Coomaraswamy, *Buddha and the Gospel of Buddhism*, p. 352; Guenon, *Man and His Becoming*, p. 25; Nikhilananda, *op. cit.*, pp. 25 ff).

[2] Swami Nikhilananda, *The Upanishads* (Harper, N.Y., 1949), vol. 1, p. 37.

cosmic frame of reference is always implied in the Indian writings.

We shall be walking in an area dealing with questions which have both proximate and ultimate meanings. However, if a journey is to be undertaken and a river is to be crossed, the important thing is to start from the near side.

CHAPTER THREE

THE NATURE OF THE SELF

'The knower and the known are one. Simple people imagine that they should see God, as if He stood there and they here. This is not so. God and I, we are one in knowledge.'—MEISTER ECKHART.

'WHO AM I?'

TWO interrelated questions are dealt with in the *Upanishads*: *Who* am I? and What is ultimately Real? These are the questions which thoughtful men everywhere ask when they have learned for themselves the drawbacks to a fragmentary living of life.

In one of the *Upanishads* a dialogue is reported between a young man, Nachiketas, and Death. The latter says to the youth: 'Take sons and grandsons, cattle and horses, elephants and gold, take a great kingdom . . . wealth, long life . . . pleasures . . . women.'

The young man replies: 'Destroyer of man! These things pass. . . . Wealth cannot satisfy a man. . . . What man, subject to death and decay, getting the chance of undecaying life, would still enjoy mere long life?' So Nachiketas chooses knowledge of *Brahman* instead of worldly success.

This story also illustrates the fundamental purpose of all the *Upanishadic* texts. They are designed to loosen man from his bondage to the transitory by pointing out the avenue to supreme knowledge. The petition of the earnest seeker is 'Lead me from the unreal to the real, lead me from darkness to light, lead me from death to immortality.'[1] Immortality here has a distinctly qualitative dimension. It is not to be equated with hope for continued personal existence in some state beyond the grave. For that state, too, according to the Indian teaching, is transitory. Immortality means knowing the Self which is unborn and undying. It is ignorance of the Self which constitutes spiritual death.

Thoughtful men everywhere have expressed something of the ambiguity of man's situation when he begins to become aware of his alienation from the Real. In the European tradition, man's spiritual dilemma has been described under the figure of the island which is apparently cut off from the mainland, though in reality the island and the mainland are one. The dominant trend in Western Christian thinking has been to develop the idea of a primordial rebellion against God. Augustine's statement of this view is the classical one. The created rational angels turned away from God, the Ground of their being, and presumed to have status in their own right. This was the sin of pride and it had its aftermath in the Garden of Eden when Adam and Eve likewise fell.

The *Upanishads* also have a story of a 'Fall'. At one time the gods had fought the demons and had obtained a victory over the latter which elated them considerably. Because of the gods' blindness they failed to recognize that it was

[1] *Brihadaranyaka Up.* 1.3.27 (F. Max Müller's translation, *Sacred Books of the East*, Clarendon Press, Oxford, 1884, vol. 15). In the case of the *Katha*, *Kena*, *Mundaka* and *Isa Upanishads*, preference has been given to the translation by Nikhilananda. A beautiful translation (partially paraphrased), without comments or verse divisions, is that by Prabhavananda and Manchester, *The Upanishads, Breath of the Eternal* (Vedanta Press, Hollywood, 1947). Cf. Teresina Rowell Havens, *Standards of Success* (Pendle Hill Pamphlet No. 43, 1948), pp. 10-11.

Brahman who had given them the victory, they themselves being mere instruments. So they bragged, 'Verily, this victory is ours; verily, this glory is ours also.' Whereupon *Brahman* appeared before them and confounded them until *Indra* through the grace of *Brahman* learned that it was only by the power of *Brahman* that the gods had won the victory.[1]

It is significant that the *Upanishads*, unlike Augustine, do not stress the note of rebellion and its dreadful consequences. Indeed, in the above tale the 'Fall' or blindness of the divine beings is not stressed so much as their subsequent illumination. In a theistic point of view (such as that of Augustine and Christendom generally), when the problem of man's alienation from the ground of his being is approached, emphasis tends to fall on the category of *will* and the virtue of *obedience*. He who disobeys the will of the priest disobeys the will of God. God's will must be made effective through legislation or coercion in one degree or another. Rebellion against the *will* becomes the cardinal sin. Higher authority has been flouted, the culprit must be punished. This may be sound moralism or good legalism, but it arises out of a superficial understanding of spiritual dynamics. By contrast, the *Upanishads* do not talk in moralistic or authoritarian terms, for theistic concepts are not regarded as ultimate. There is no mention of man rebelling against the gods. Man is not a 'sinner' who has turned against the gods; he has, rather, lost sight of his true good and suffers from *avidya* (unawareness). What man needs is not 'pardon' but *vidya* (awareness).

Why does man *ignore* his real nature? The predicament is

[1] *Kena Up.* 3.1-12; 4.1.

traceable to *maya*. *Maya* is strictly untranslatable although 'illusion' is the term most commonly used by Western students. This is definitely misleading. *Maya* is inscrutable; it comes into being and it passes away. It is the world of appearances rather than the world of reality; or, to state it in a slightly different way, the world of reality as seen from a finite point of view. Coomaraswamy points out that the doctrine of *maya* does not assert the insignificance of the world but stresses that *as we see the world*, 'extended in the order of space, time and causality, it has no static existence as a thing in itself: our partial vision is false in so far, and *only in so far*, as it is partial'.[1] The world has as much significance as the degree of a man's enlightenment allows him to discover in it. If man becomes unduly bewitched by the world, he will not gain Self-knowledge.

THE RAZOR'S EDGE

The way to Self-knowledge is as narrow as the sharp edge of a razor, hard to tread and difficult to cross. The desired insight cannot be gained through knowledge of the physical world nor through intellectual analysis. Beyond a certain stage in the search, the analytical mind must be stopped completely.[2] However, the preliminary stages call for control of the senses and a discriminating mind.

If the senses are not checked by a discriminating mind, the individual becomes bound ever more closely to an unsatisfying, transient round of existence. The world of *maya* can also be described as the realm of *samsara*. *Samsara* means

[1] Coomaraswamy, *Buddha and the Gospel of Buddhism*, pp. 210-11.
[2] Cf. *Katha Up.* 1.3.13-14.

'stream', i.e. stream of existences.[1] Actually *samsara* is the realm of flux and becoming—the realm where man lives. It is the only place where man has an opportunity to find the meaning of life. Any other existences which man may transmigrate into after death are only temporary. Each must stay in the 'stream' until he has found the further shore—namely union with the highest Reality.[2]

The doctrine of *samsara* has frequently been interpreted as a doctrine of despair by Western students. Actually it is a doctrine of hope when contrasted with the Christian teaching on the eternal torment of the damned. This Christian teaching is an unequivocal doctrine of pessimism. It implies that the majority of the human race are not teachable, meriting torment of an 'infinite' duration for a finite period of sinning. Augustine, in one of his speculative moods, suggested that God would save only enough souls to even up the ranks of the angels depleted when the angels had originally rebelled against God under the leadership of Satan. The Protestant reformer Calvin taught that God gave just enough light to the heathen to insure their damnation. Over against this 'one life—one chance' theory of salvation, the Hindu doctrine of *samsara* stresses the many chances which each being has to achieve its desired goal. This feeling of the

[1] '. . . The constitution of worlds and of individuals is compared to a wheel . . . the "wheel of becoming, or birth". . . . The collective motion of all the wheels within wheels . . . that are these worlds and individuals is called the Confluence (*samsara*), and it is in this "storm of the world's flow" that our "elemental self" is fatally involved.' Coomaraswamy, *Hinduism and Buddhism*, p. 16.

[2] Radhakrishnan, *Indian Philosophy* (Macmillan, N.Y., 1929), vol. 1, p. 250. For early passages on transmigration idea, see *Chandogya Up.* 5.3.10; *Brihadaranyaka Up.* 6.2. Cf. article 'Transmigration' (Buddhist), by M. Anesaki in Hasting's *Encyclopedia of Religion and Ethics*, vol. 12.

oneness of all life is just as much a part of the Indian tradition as the desire to escape the realm of transiency and becoming.

The concept of *samsara* is closely related to the *law of karma* in *Upanishadic* thought. All actions are included in the operation of this *karmic* law. Whatever is sown must be reaped, sometime and somewhere. Every action produces its effects. As the *Brihadaranyaka Upanishad* says, 'A man becomes good by good deeds and bad by bad deeds.' Each person is responsible for producing the desired change in his *karma*. According to what a man wills today, so will he be tomorrow.[1] What each person is today is the result of past actions and attitudes, plus any modifications introduced through his own will. Unfortunately the average person, caught in the toils of his *karma*, dragged under in the 'stream', looks at life in terms of its opposites. The most misleading pair of opposites (misleading because it is highly undependable as a safe guide beyond a certain minimal stage) is that of pleasure versus pain.[2]

PLEASURE VERSUS PAIN

Any person who is primarily aware of his own confusion or frustration finds it hard to concentrate on the question of the larger good. When one is sick, he simply wants to be well. He may forget that when he was well, he was still dissatisfied and restless. Man is frequently much more aware of what he wants to be free *from* than what he wants to be freed *for*. Part of this inability to comprehend what the

[1] *Brihadaranyaka Up*. 3.2.13; *Chandogya Up*. 3.14.1.

[2] The concept of *karma* receives a more detailed treatment in the chapter on the *Bhagavad Gita* and the chapters dealing with Buddhism.

larger good may be arises from the fact that man tends to think and respond to life in terms of the opposites, pleasure and pain.

The child is a naïve hedonist for a long time. He seeks to avoid painful states or conditions and clamours for certain pleasurable satisfactions. He has no philosophy about it whatsoever. But there comes a time when the child discovers he must choose between competing pleasures or pains. This involves hard choice, a weighing of present pleasure against postponed pleasure. The child is father to the man and the man frequently tries to work out a 'hedonic calculus'. In the attempt to devise a graded chart of competing pleasure-claims and pain-claims, man gets hopelessly involved. His pleasure-yardstick just will not operate satisfactorily. Too many factors are at work over which he has no control. Furthermore, one day's pleasure may be the next day's displeasure.

In this predicament a man may decide to make the best of a poor bargain. Admitting the inadequacy of his own 'controls', he more or less resentfully puts up with the painful facts of existence. On the other hand, a person may decide to forgo some of his present pleasures, which are being denied to him in any event, in return for expected rewards in Heaven. This is the pathway followed by many people in all of the world religions.

The *Upanishads* are very critical of this postponing of pleasures to the 'Great Hereafter'. Hedonism is still hedonism even though sensuous or material pleasures have been rebaptized and called heavenly pleasures. To postpone today's pleasures because they are unattainable (either because of outer circumstances or inner confusion) in the expectation of having them tomorrow, may be evidence of consummate skill or cool worldly strategy that pays off in small amounts. It is not evidence of significant spiritual growth.

The *Katha Upanishad* states that even the highest heaven (*Brahmaloka*) must be renounced by the man who desires genuine Self-knowledge.[1] For the pleasant and the good are two dissimilar yardsticks. The pleasant serves one set of needs at a certain level; its opposite, pain, is always lurking in the background. Pursuit of the pleasant binds a man to specific duties, to studied disciplines and institutional practices, to rigidities in conduct and attitude. The person continues to believe that by persisting in such disciplines he will be able to achieve the anticipated pleasures. Yet the harder he strives, the more tense he becomes and the less capable of reaching his goal.

This lies back of such *Upanishadic* statements that Self-realization cannot be obtained by the study of the *Vedas*, or by intelligence, or by much hearing of sacred books. Nor can it be obtained through 'religious works'. Frail indeed are the sacrificial rafts which are supposed to carry one from the shore of ignorance to the shore of Self-knowledge. World desires are a barrier whether one desires the pleasant things of this world or of some world hereafter. The supreme good is one thing, the pleasant another.[2]

Whence this confusion between the good and the pleasant? Why does pursuit of the fragmentary objects of the senses or of the intellect in its analytical processes condemn man to a life of restlessness, dissatisfaction and bondage to the realm

[1] *Katha Up.* 1.2.9-10, with commentary.

[2] *Ibid.* 1.2.1, 23; *Mundaka Up.* 1.2.7. Cf. *Katha Up.* 1.2.10 ff, where there is implied a succession of steps in the life of desire.

of *samsara*? Augustine's analysis of man's dilemma is somewhat more familiar to Occidentals. At one point it is very close to the analysis of the *Upanishads*. According to Augustine, man is doomed to perpetual dissatisfaction because he is trying to satisfy an infinite need with finite sops. Man is made for union with God, but because of his 'fallen' condition, he pursues the objects of sense in ways that are foredoomed to be self-frustrating. This inability to achieve genuine satisfactions through following the senses Augustine termed lust.

The *Upanishadic* description of man's predicament is very similar. Man, designed for knowledge of the Supreme, lives a life of distractedness. He is caught in a net of bewilderment. Having intimations of an entire grove of trees before him to explore, still he clings tenaciously to a small shrub. 'Intoxicated by the wine of illusion . . ., rushing about like one possessed by an evil spirit; bitten by the world like one bitten by a great serpent; darkened by passion like the night', he stays under the sway of *maya*.[1]

Man's spiritual problem is resolved neither by 'religion' nor by social service. For so long as man's actions are done in Self-ignorance, the rewards are purely temporary and the results are quite mixed.[2] People who follow these paths are like children, immersed in ignorance and flattering themselves, saying, 'We have accomplished life's purpose.' Such people may be happy in a superficial way, yet part of the price of their blindness is the unexpected ending of their

[1] Cf. *Maitrayani Up*. 7.8; 4.2.

[2] 'Ignorant fools, regarding sacrifices and humanitarian works as the highest, do not know any higher good. Having enjoyed their reward on the heights of heaven, gained by good works, they enter again this world or a lower one.' *Mundaka Up*. 1.2.10.

momentary state of joy. For they are still in bondage to the transient and have not sought the larger good. 'Dwelling in darkness, but wise in their own conceit and puffed up with vain scholarship', they wander about 'being afflicted by many ills, like blind men led by the blind'.[1]

The roots of this blindness lie within. Each man must take the appropriate steps for himself. This blindness is akin to that which leads a man to mistake a shadow lurking in the darkness for a wild animal about to attack, when in reality it is a tree stump; or to mistake a mirage in the desert for a pool of cooling water. So long as one ignorantly identifies the real self with fragmented desires, one remains as it were in 'the jaws of death'. However, man need not despair, for all life moves towards its Self-actualization: 'All go towards the tree intended for their abode, so all this goes to the Supreme Self.'[2]

If one is to realize his highest potential, he must learn how to exercise discrimination. For one thing, the senses must not be allowed to lead one into further involvement or distractions by roaming around uncontrolled 'like the vicious horses of a charioteer'. The body is a vehicle which must be kept in proper condition and under proper guidance. In the figure of the *Katha Upanishad*, the body is the chariot, the horses are the senses, the charioteer is the discriminative faculty, the mind is the reins, and the master of the chariot is the Self (*Atman*).[3] The man of discrimination does not allow the horses to run away with the chariot. Unless one learns how to control the senses, he will not be able to go on to the next

[1] *Mundaka Up.* 1.2.9; 1.2.8.; cf. *Katha Up.* 1.2.12.

[2] *Katha Up.* 1.3.15; *Prasna Up.* 4.7.

[3] *Katha Up.* 1.3, 5-9.

step which is that of controlling the wandering mind and the analytical intellect.[1] Since controlling the senses is not an end in itself, it is necessary to push a little further our inquiry into what is meant by the *Upanishadic* saying that the true seeker after Self-knowledge must be 'free from all desires'.

'FREE FROM ALL DESIRES'

The teaching on desirelessness cannot be taken literally by the novice. The *Chandogya Upanishad* makes a distinction between 'true desires' and 'false desires': 'These true desires, however, are hidden by what is false; though the desires be true, they have a covering which is false.' Another writing states, 'Desire is never satisfied by the enjoyment of the objects of desire; it grows more and more as does the fire to which fuel is added.'[2] In this case craving, or blind desire, is being described. Blind (or false) desires are both compulsive and compensatory. They are compulsive in that the person has no real control over their overt expression. They are compensatory in that they are masquerading for some other need of the human organism. They do not lead the person on toward Self-knowledge because they fixate the person's attention unduly upon the world at a superficial level.

The spiritually alert person desires 'nothing but what he ought to desire'. This is because both the senses and the mind have been tranquillized or stilled. The threat to Self-knowledge is not the external world but the tendency to *dwell* on worldly objects or long for specific pleasures either here or hereafter. Serene persons, says the *Katha Upanishad*,

[1] This latter step is very important, and is dealt with in more detail in chapters 4 and 7.

[2] *Chandogya Up.* 8.3.1.; cf. 8.2.5-6. *Laws of Manu*, 2.94.

'do not covet any uncertain thing in the world'. Coveting arises from non-awareness; it is the result of misusing the external world. Self-knowledge and craving are thus at opposite poles.

This Self-knowledge is not inconsistent with life *in* the world, but one must not be *of* the world. An *Upanishadic* passage cited frequently by Indians, especially those in the householder stage, states: 'It is not for the sake of the husband, my dear, that the husband is loved, but for the sake of the Self that he is loved.' [1] All things and all relationships should be regarded as instruments of Self-realization. This does not mean that other persons are to be used as means in a purely utilitarian sense. That would be to exploit another. But all persons and all relationships are significant means to an all-inclusive end. Through right discrimination, each person is helped on in his search for release from fragmentariness—that is, *moksha*.

LIBERATION OR FREEDOM

Moksha means very simply *release*—release from finitude, fragmentariness and unawareness. The concept has often been caricatured in the West. This is partly because of the use of the misleading word 'absorption' with reference to it. Absorption has primarily physical connotations to physically minded moderns.

While *moksha* means release from the round of birth and death, this is only the negative way of stating a positive good—release from bondage into freedom. The release is from something finite and thwarting into a condition of joy.

[1] *Brihadaranyaka Up*. 2.4.5.

The Indian tradition makes it quite clear that such an experience of release can be obtained here and now. The *Upanishads* describe the freed person as one who traverses these worlds eating whatever food he likes, taking whatever forms he likes, joyously singing songs. The expansion of spirit is definitely exhilarating. 'A man who is free from desire beholds the majesty of the Self through tranquillity of the senses and the mind and becomes free from grief', says the *Katha Upanishad.* Such a person is no longer bothered by hunger, thirst, sorrow or confusion. He does not worry about old age and death. He experiences 'the delight of life and mind, the fullness of peace and eternity'.[1] The Indians describe the person who has achieved such a state as blessed.

It is taught that each man has the capacity for achieving this condition. It is hidden in the heart of all living creatures. Each must come to this intuitive Self-knowledge by himself, through certain disciplines. No one else can do it for him, but one should have a tutor or guide. The ideal tutor (or *guru*) is the person who is himself liberated.[2] The *guru* undoubtedly served in many cases as a personalized object of devotion. Students served their teacher as devout servants serve their lord. The student helped to supply the minimal physical needs of the teacher. This included gathering wood for the *guru's* fire. The teacher became the nucleus for those seeking a similar goal. His home became a fellowship of like-minded seekers.

Important as the teacher was as a tutor and guide, each person had to travel his own inner path to Self-knowledge.

[1] *Katha Up.* 1.2.20; 2.3.14-15; *Taittiriyaka Up.* 3.10.8.

[2] *Katha Up.* 1.2.20, 21; 1.2.7-8.

Whenever such insight was achieved, it was described as 'a flash of lightning' or 'a wink of the eye'. He who reached it might be able to help others in the preliminary stages, but he left no path. As one commentator puts it, 'The knower of *Brahman* leaves behind no footprint by which he can be traced. "As a bird flies in the air, as a fish moves in the water, without leaving any trace, so likewise the illumined soul leaves behind no footprint."'[1] The man who learns how to swim may be able to assist another, but he cannot swim for him.

WORSHIP IN THE HIGHER SENSE

The sense of wholeness which Indians describe as the union of *Atman* with *Brahman* can be realized in the present. It is not discovered in patches or in fragments, but is known in every state of mind. It is an all-pervasive kind of experience. Worship for such a person is no longer primarily something done on a visible altar. Every act of the illumined person is an act of worship. So-called objective worship (the worship of a divine object or entity) has disappeared from the picture.

This emphasis is underscored in various parts of the *Upanishads*. The *Brihadaranyaka* says, 'If a man worships another divinity with the idea that he and the God are different, he does not know.'[2] If a man claims to know *Brahman* as an object of knowledge, he does not know *Brahman*, but some idea or construct about it. *Brahman* is never 'Object' yet is involved in every search for meaning or cosmic reintegration. In the words of the *Kena Upanishad*, 'That

[1] *Kena Up.* 4.4. Cf. Nikhilananda, *op. cit.*, p. 307.

[2] Cf. *Mundaka Up.* 2.1.10; 3.2.6.; *Kena Up.* 2.4.

which cannot be expressed by speech, but by which speech is expressed—That alone know as *Brahman*, and not that which people here worship.' [1]

There are places where the *Upanishads* make concessions to the common man's forms of worship, where *Brahman* is regarded as having 'form'.[2] Such worship, however, is described as representing the lower path. Or, changing the figure, frail indeed are the boats which such worshippers use in trying to cross *samsara*, the stream of ordinary life. For altar, icon or creed become relatively unimportant to the man who has come 'in the twinkling of an eye' to Self-knowledge. In some incommunicable sense altar, worshipper and worshipped become unified: 'That art Thou.'

To try to describe in traditional Western theological terms what is involved here is impossible. For most of those terms are dualistic—nature versus supernature, man versus God, flesh versus spirit, law versus grace, faith versus works. If one is to understand even in part what the *Upanishads* are saying, one must come out of the cloister dedicated to theological dualism. The dynamic terms of Western psychology can be a very partial aid. But one must go to the seers and poets, to the giants of the mystical tradition of the West, to develop real feeling for the Eastern viewpoint. As Meister Eckhart has said regarding the search for the supreme identity, 'To get at the core of God at his greatest, one must first get into the core of himself at his least, for no one can

[1] *Kena Up.* 1.5; 1.7-9. Cf. A. W. Watts, *The Supreme Identity*, pp. 52, 78, 87.

[2] The *Taittiriyaka Upanishad* says, 'Let him worship *Brahman* as support and he becomes supported. Let him worship *Brahman* as mind, he becomes endowed with mind. And let him worship *Brahman* as *Brahman*, and he becomes possessed of *Brahman*.' *Taittiriyaka Up.* 3.10.

know God who has not first known himself. Go to the depths of the soul . . . to the root, to the heights; for all that God can do is focused there.' [1]

He who undertakes such an exploration with all the intelligence and will he can muster may begin to understand worship in its higher sense. Like the *Upanishadic* sage he may discover that altars, icons and creeds are only pointers on the path leading to Self-realization.

[1] R. Blakney, *Meister Eckhart: A Modern Translation*, p. 246.

CHAPTER FOUR

THE ART OF YOGA

'The seed of God is in us. Given an intelligent and hard-working farmer, it will thrive and grow up to God, whose seed it is; and accordingly its fruits will be God-nature. Pear seeds grow into pear trees, nut seeds into nut trees, and God seed into God.'—MEISTER ECKHART.

EVERY man at times has intimations of a larger awareness than he has yet realized. Not every person finds it possible to discover the specific techniques suited to him which will lead to that actualization. Most people would readily agree that a house divided against itself cannot stand securely for long. The tensions can become unendurable; one either takes drugs or his life.

The acute question is: How can the inner split be overcome in such a way as to lead to renewed life and an enlarged awareness of meaning or purpose? Many people do actually settle for some kind of temporary relief from the painful symptoms which bother them, instead of trying to extend their area of awareness. Since in Indian circles it was assumed that *only in this world could man achieve his final freedom*, a great deal of thought was given to the refining of those tools or disciplines which would assure one of realizing liberation or *moksha*.[1]

[1] Cf. *Mundaka Up.* 1.2.10. For an excellent critique of the assumption that this 'middle world' is the only place where genuine spiritual development can proceed, see Gerald Heard, *Preface to Prayer* (Harper, N.Y., 1944), section on 'The Universal and the Topical in Brahmanic-Buddhistic Cosmology'.

YOGA—THE REINTEGRATION OF THE SELF

It is fruitless to discuss the historical question as to when *yoga* was first introduced into Indian life. Excavations at Mohenjo-daro have unearthed a seal (dated around 3000 B.C.) which shows a four-faced figure seated with legs folded in *yogi*-like posture, the posture traditionally associated with the state of contemplation. Around the seated figure are four beasts—the bull, elephant, buffalo and rhinoceros. This suggests the conclusion that the god later known as Siva, the Great Yogi (*Maha-yogin*), was worshipped by the pre-Aryan people of Mohenjo-daro in the aspect of *Pasupati*, Lord of Beasts.[1] Contrary to the claims of many Western interpreters, this suggests that *yoga* disciplines are much older than the written *Vedas* and *Upanishads*.

The literal meaning of the word *yoga* is 'to yoke'. The reference in the last chapter to the horses being held in check by the charioteer is of prime importance here. The horses (man's sensitive powers) must be yoked lest they draw man away from his ultimate goal, which is spiritual union. Thus the word has a two-fold meaning: it stands for the ultimate realization of the union (*yoga*) of *Atman* and *Brahman*. It also stands for the methods or disciplines preparatory to that union. While the union between *Atman* and *Brahman* exists potentially or virtually in every man, each individual has to become conscious of *that which truly is from all eternity*.

[1] Dorothy Mackay, *Mohenjo-daro and the Ancient Civilization of the Indus Valley* (Annual Report of the Smithsonian Institution, 1932), p. 435. See Plate M, 9, in Ernest Mackay, *The Indus Civilization*, after p. 202. Sir John Marshall claims that the seated figure is Siva (*Mohenjo-daro and the Indus Civilization*, Probsthain, London, 1932, 3 vols.).

Each man must 'yoke himself like an understanding horse'.[1] This has reference both to man's mental and physical powers.

Yoga methods are a characteristic feature of Indian religion.[2] To some extent every Hindu is a practitioner of *yoga*, as the chapter on *The Teachings of the Gita* will make clearer. But when it comes to the more intensive forms of contemplation, as Coomaraswamy has pointed out, a good many special exercises are involved, and at any given time probably only a small minority of people are engaged in them. The preparatory phases for this intensive activity involve moral preparation, physical exercises, complete control of the breathing process. All of these are necessary before one proceeds far with the purely mental exercises.

The charge is sometimes made that *yoga* is nothing more than a pathological variety of asceticism or an escape from the complexity of life. Some of those who make this criticism speak as though almost any form of self-restraint is unhealthy. This may be traceable in part to a post-Victorian reaction against unhealthy forms of 'Puritanism' which sought to repress certain drives or tendencies instead of understanding or transcending them. In any event, in some circles over-indulgence has come to be the acceptable virtue in place of conventionalized (and frequently dishonest) restraint. The devotees of the cult of indulgence are slow to recognize that it too is a form of self-torture, no more emancipating in the

[1] Guenon, *Man and His Becoming*, p. 38; *Rig Veda* V.46.1; Coomaraswamy, *Hinduism and Buddhism*, p. 40.

[2] Occidentals need to remember that public demonstrators of so-called *yogic* powers are regarded as misguided pilgrims by serious Indians. At worst, such persons are charlatans catering to the curiosity-seekers.

long run than Victorian prudishness. It produces its own plentiful supply of hair-shirts with no transcendent goal offered to make the wearing of the shirt less painful. The self-indulgent man lies down to sleep, but not to rest. The self-restraints practised by the *yogin* at least aim at tranquillity rather than further agitation, concentration rather than distractedness. His restraint has a higher end in view than restraint; whereas indulgence has no higher end than further indulgence.

At the present time the Occident is in a position where it may be able to reassess the meaning and value of *yoga* methods. Western interest in the subject of psychology and psychoanalysis can possibly be diverted into an exploration of the deeper ranges of Eastern metaphysic.[1] To Freud goes much of the credit for making contemporary Western man psychologically self-conscious. The resemblance between psychoanalysis and the preliminary phases of *yoga* has been aptly commented on by Alan W. Watts. 'The first phase of *yoga* consists in distinguishing the Seer from the seen, the *via negativa* of realizing that the Self *is not* any known object. Likewise, psychoanalysis aims to know the unconscious objectively. It makes us aware that what we project is actually within ourselves, but the moment we recognize anything within ourselves, we have distinguished it from the knowing Self. The practical function of psychoanalysis is to heal the soul—that is, to get the *whole* psyche into consciousness. For while some part of the psyche is unconscious, that is, identified with the Self, it causes confused and unobjective reactions to life. For example, when we are un-

[1] Cf. Geraldine Coster, *Yoga and Western Psychology* (Oxford Univ. Press, London, 1945).

conscious of our own hostility, we project hostile motives upon others, and so fail to establish rapport with them.'[1]

The major drawback to the usual psychoanalytic treatment is that it 'does not plumb the unconscious deeply enough to reveal the Self and get it fully distinguished from the ego'; thus 'it does not proceed, with *yoga*, to understand the identity of the Self with the infinite'. It is too concerned with a finite operation, a specific terminus such as 'adjusting' the person to a particular environment as though that were the highest good.[2]

THE YOGA SUTRA OF PATANJALI

The basic assumption of Indian *yoga* is that there is a wider world about us than we normally apprehend. This wider world does not include only that region termed the sub-conscious in the West, but also a level of consciousness extending beyond the normal waking states. The Indian experimenters sought to chart something of the pathway to that level of *superconsciousness*.[3]

The oldest literary source describing *yoga* methods in some

[1] A. W. Watts, *The Supreme Identity*, pp. 89-90.

[2] American books on how to sleep, how to extend one's memory, how to relax, etc., are a form of pseudo-*yoga*. They tend to be based on the assumption that the end of life is in terms of charm, money-making, or 'personality'. The goods and goals of a commercial society are taken quite seriously. This emphasis on a *via affirmativa* of an advertiser's paradise is hardly adequate preparation for the *via negativa* wherein one learns to deny himself and, if need be, his particular society, in order to discover the values that are eternal.

[3] For an introduction to Hindu psychology and *yoga*, see Swami Akhilananda, *Hindu Psychology* (Harper, N.Y., 1946).

detail is the *Yoga Sutra* of Patanjali.[1] With Patanjali, *yoga* stands for the path of strenuous endeavour by which one restrains the senses and the mind. The main emphasis is on the methodical steps in the discipline. The *Sutra* represents the crystallization of many ideas and practices. Patanjali specifies three stages in the discipline. All rest back on the close connection between the mind and the body in Indian thought. The embodied self is made up of three strands (*gunas*). One strand or component (the *sattva guna*) expresses itself as tranquillity of mind, calmness of spirit, purity of desire. The second component (the *rajas guna*) expresses itself as aggressive activity, restlessness, passion. The third factor (the *tamas guna*) manifests itself as laziness, inertia and stupidity. In varying degrees these three elements are present in each person. Each must seek to rise from the level of *tamas*, through the life of action to the level of *sattva*, where one is attached only to the pursuit of wisdom and inner tranquillization.

It is the aim of *yoga* discipline, first, to overcome *tamas* by *rajas* and then to overcome *rajas* through *sattva*. If the superficial layers of consciousness are to be cut open so that the inner Self may be realized, there must be ethical preparation. This is the first stage in the discipline. One must abstain from injuring any living creature, from lying, theft, incontinence and avarice. Non-injury means one must refrain not only from overt violence but also from hatred.[2] Those who

[1] It has been dated all the way from the second century B.C. to the third century A.D. Cf. Radhakrishnan, *Indian Philosophy*, vol. 2, pp. 341-342, on the critical question. See Introduction by J. H. Woods to Patanjali's Yoga Sutras (Harvard Oriental Series, vol. 17, Cambridge, 1927).

[2] *Yoga Sutra* II.20, 31, 34.

commit themselves seriously to the path of *yoga* must also practise five observances: purification, contentment, austerity, study and devotion to *Isvara* (God-as-personal).[1] These ethical preparations are required regardless of time or place or race.

The second stage involves bodily aids—posture, breath-control, withdrawal of the senses from the objects—designed to prepare the mind for single-mindedness. The body must be in a convenient posture before meditation can begin. Breathing exercises have been emphasized by the devotees of *Hatha yoga*, though Patanjali mentions it as an optional matter.[2] (*Hatha yoga* tends to concentrate on the cultivation of special psychophysical powers, sometimes to the neglect of the larger spiritual goal.)

Withdrawal of the senses from the objective world is a most important indirect aid to contemplation. To hold the wandering mind, even for a matter of seconds, is very difficult, as simple experimentation shows. That complete mastery of the 'mind-stuff' was not simple even for Indians is indicated by the four kinds of *incomplete* mastery listed by the commentators on *Yoga Sutra* II.55. There were apparently some who assumed they had achieved complete mastery simply when there was an absence of desire for various things. Others held that attachment to things not specifically forbidden by the sacred writings was no hindrance to complete mastery. A third group claimed that one could legitimately enjoy any of the objects of sense so long as one was not dependent upon them. Still others asserted that the senses were properly 'withdrawn' or subjugated when one could

1 *Yoga Sutra* II.32; I.23.

2 *Ibid.* I.33-34. Cf. Akhilananda, *op. cit.*, pp. 186-7, on *Hatha yoga*.

think about passion or aversion without pleasure or pain. All of these masteries of the wandering senses as reflected in the mind are incomplete, for they are still in contact with objects-of-sense. As such they are dangerous. 'Even a man who knows the lore of poisons and who is a perfect master of serpents does not take a serpent on his lap and quietly go to sleep.' [1] The only complete mastery is when there is singleness-of-intent, following upon the closing of the door of the mind to all sense impressions.

All of these preparations are a prelude to the third stage which begins with fixed-attention and goes on to contemplation or *samadhi* (frequently translated superconsciousness: it is the state of *union*, that is, *yoga*). The Self has now completely realized its oneness with ultimate Reality, *Brahman*. No description of this highest state can be given; one must experience it for himself.

> *By* yoga, yoga *must be known,*
> Yoga *increaseth* yoga's *store.*
> *He who for* yoga *care hath shown*
> *In* yoga *rests for evermore.*[2]

However, the *Chandogya Upanishad* suggests a clue to the meaning of this unitive state. *Indra* and *Virokana* are represented as coming to *Prajapati* for instruction concerning the Self. They desire to know the Self that is free from sin, old age, death, grief, hunger and thirst; the Self 'which desires nothing but what it ought to desire'.[3] *Prajapati* first tells them

[1] *Yoga Sutra* II.55, with Vyasa's comment and the explanation by Vachaspati-Mishra.

[2] *Yoga Bhashya* III.6.

[3] *Chandogya Up.* 8.7.1.

to look at their reflections in the water, to see whether they can see the Self. They understand him to mean that the real Self is the body which is reflected in the water. *Indra* returns dissatisfied, pointing out that the body is not fearless, free from hunger, old age, or death. *Prajapati* then proceeds to give the second lesson about the Self. 'He who moves about happy in dreams', says *Prajapati*, 'he is the Self; this is the immortal, the fearless; this is *Brahman*.' *Indra* meditates on this, mindful of the fact that in the dream state the person moves about with a great deal of freedom from restricting conditions. Then he remembers that one can be quite conscious of pain, tears and struggle in a dream. 'I see no good in this', he comments, and returns for his third instruction.

Prajapati then proceeds to give *Indra* the lesson for which he is now ready. 'When a man falls asleep, reposing, and at perfect rest, sees no dreams, that is the Self; this is the immortal, the fearless; this is *Brahman*.' This teaching implies to *Indra* that the Self has 'gone to utter annihilation'. *Prajapati* then explains to him the significance of the simile of deep sleep: In deep sleep there is no duality; the distinction of subject and object falls away; there is no sense of struggle nor of pleasure and pain. Hence the state of dreamless sleep provides a clue to the meaning of *samadhi*, or superconsciousness.[1] In this state there is a complete suspension of all ordinary faculties. After one has emerged from it there remains the intuition of a state of consciousness which eludes all description, even as one who sleeps without dreams cannot describe what has happened in the interval.[2]

[1] *Chandoga Up*. 8.7.1-12; 6.8.1-2.

[2] Cf. Watts, *op. cit*., p. 152 n.

YOGAS FOR DIFFERENT TEMPERAMENTS

Patanjali's interpretation of *yoga* was out of the reach of the average man—the farmer, the hewer of wood, the drawer of water. It was a 'royal path' (*Raja yoga*). The members of the mercantile and peasant castes could rarely spare the time for the prolonged periods of meditation possible to an upper-caste person. The masses of India were to follow a much broader path—*bhakti yoga* combined with *karma yoga. Bhakti yoga* usually is described as the pathway of faith or loving devotion.[1] It is a path familiar to many in the tradition of evangelical Christianity and popular Catholicism: one finds salvation through devotion to Jesus as personal lord and saviour. The cardinal feature of *bhakti yoga* is that Reality is thought of in highly concrete, personal, even erotic terms. The worshipper gives himself in loving devotion to his Beloved.

Patanjali had introduced the idea of a personal God (*Isvara*) in the first section of his *Yoga Sutras*.[2] It was not indispensable to the rest of his system. Yet many Indians were to use just such a concept to aid them in overcoming the obstacles to spiritual realization. For those living in families and earning a living in the market-places, devotion to a personal God came to be the most commonly travelled way.

During the earlier period of the priestly commentaries, the *Brahmanas*, *karma yoga* had stood for the way of 'ritual' works. Before the production of the *Bhagavad Gita*, it had come to stand for the way of right action. In the *Gita*, *karma yoga* is combined with *bhakti yoga*: every action is to be done

[1] *Bhakti*, derived from the root *bhaj*, to serve.

[2] *Yoga Sutra* I.23 ff.

with devotion. The continuing popularity of the *Gita* indicates that the high ideal of spirituality set forth in the traditional Indian teaching is meaningful to the common man, who must, however, find his Self-realization in the midst of his work. This world is not the Real world, yet it is the finite arena within which one can find the Self that transcends the world.

CHAPTER FIVE

TEACHINGS OF THE BHAGAVAD GITA

'The world is a bridge. Pass over it but do not build upon it.'—From the Persian.

TRUTH is not something which can be captured 'once and for all' as rain water is caught in a vessel. Nor is it something which can be passed on externally by way of indoctrination. That is to substitute a husk for the reality. Each person must go to experience to find the truth of life. Whatever tradition or culture has nourished a person, it has done its educational job well only if it has evoked from him potentialities that were waiting to be quickened into expression. Radhakrishnan has well said that 'a tradition is authentic when it evokes an adequate response to the reality represented by it. It is valid when our minds thrill and vibrate to it. When it fails to achieve this end, new teachers arise to rekindle it.' Coomaraswamy adds that 'there cannot be an absolute truth which is not accessible to direct experience'.[1]

Interpretations of highest truth will change as generations

[1] S. Radhakrishnan, *The Bhagavad Gita* (Harper, N.Y., 1948), p. 151; Coomaraswamy, *Buddha and the Gospel of Buddhism*, p. 237, n. 1. Radhakrishnan's translation includes the Sanskrit text of the *Gita* in Romanized letters, and is divided into verses. Hence it has certain advantages for the new student. However, its notes may sometimes be confusing. The translation by Swami Prabhavananda and Christopher Isherwood (*Bhagavad-Gita*, Marcel Rodd, Hollywood, 1944) can be highly recommended as a parallel study; it can be read much more easily than either Radhakrishnan's or Nikhilananda's. See Bibliography at end.

come and go. This means that tradition is always being transcended as the timeless truth is being realized. Growth in insight is an ongoing process, dynamic in its nature. The *Bhagavad Gita* [1] was the result of the appearance of new teachers who sought to state man's spiritual nature and destiny in fresh terms appropriate to the age. The *Gita* is called the most important single work ever produced in India. It is a compendium of the whole *Vedic* doctrine. In eighteen chapters a dialogue is carried on between Arjuna, a member of the warrior caste of ancient India, and Lord Krishna, a personal incarnation of deity. The dialogue is contained within the great Indian epic known as the *Mahabharata*.[2] Many Indian commentators have pointed out that it is not a specific chapter in one man's history that is being described here. Rather is it the history of every man.[3]

TO ACT OR NOT TO ACT?

The story opens with Arjuna hesitant and despondent on the field of battle. A fratricidal war is about to begin in

[1] 'The Divine Song', or 'Song of the Lord'.

[2] On the basis of its archaic constructions and internal references, Radhakrishnan assigns the *Gita* to the fifth century B.C., but he admits the text may have received many alterations in subsequent centuries (*op. cit.*, p. 14; cf. his *Indian Philosophy*, vol. 1, pp. 522-5). For a critical discussion of the original *Gita*, relation of the *Gita* to the *Mahabharata*, to the *Upanishads*, etc., see S. C. Roy, *The Bhagavad-Gita and Modern Scholarship* (Luzac, London, 1941); Rudolf Otto, *The Original Gita* (Allen & Unwin, London, 1939).

[3] In the Vaishnava scriptures the worshipper of Krishna is instructed that the story of Krishna is not a history but a process continuously unfolded in the heart of man. (Coomaraswamy says that the pseudo-historical Krishna and Arjuna are to be identified with the mythical *Agni* and *Indra*. Coomaraswamy, *Hinduism and Buddhism*, p. 5; cf. *Buddha and the Gospel of Buddhism*, p. 236.)

which brother will be slaying brother. Before the actual outbreak of the fighting, Arjuna, who has stationed his chariot between the two armies in order to have a comprehensive view, suddenly loses heart. He turns to Krishna, his charioteer, and confesses that he cannot go through with it. 'My mind is reeling. . . . Nor do I foresee any good by slaying my own people in the fight. I do not long for victory, O Krishna, nor kingdom nor pleasure.' [1] His limbs fail him, his mouth goes dry, his bow slips from his hand. Arjuna is ready to toss in the sponge.

The dilemma of Arjuna is the dilemma of every man, the commentators point out. Realizing in a moment of clarity the ambiguous situation in which he is enmeshed, he sees the contradictory impulses which have ruled him to the present. Caught in the rip-tide of outer circumstances and emerging insights, he loses his native assurance. What he has been accustomed to doing now seems for the first time to be impossible. Seeing routine actions and duties in a new light, he loses his nerve. Confronted with the realization that he has missed life's real goal, his initial reaction is a desire for flight, withdrawal for time for reflection.

After the statement of the problem in the first chapter, the remaining seventeen chapters of the *Gita* are devoted to the line of reasoning which Lord Krishna is represented as using to persuade Arjuna that there is no escape through withdrawal.

THE PREDICAMENT ANALYSED

Since the conflict is an inner one, one cannot flee the field of battle. One must accept the conflict and seek to win

[1] I.30-32.

through to illumination. Each person is a battleground where opposite forces meet. In experience nothing is wholly good or wholly evil. In each man there is the godlike mind and the demoniac mind. The endowments of the godlike mind are steadfastness in knowledge, charity, self-control, forgiveness, freedom from malice and related tendencies. The demoniac mind, on the other hand, is expressed in arrogance, excessive pride, anger, avarice. These latter tendencies all make for increasing bondage; the former point in the direction of deliverance.[1] Only when one comes to see for himself that the demoniac mind is the result of identification of the real Self with what is partial and fragmentary is there genuine deliverance. The real Self must become single-minded. 'The resolute understanding is single; but the thoughts of the irresolute are many-branched and endless.' [2] This distractedness is the symptom of one's having wandered away from home.

The *Gita* follows the *Upanishadic* teaching that the real Self, or *Atman*, is not to be equated with the embodied or fragmented self. Commentators on the *Gita's* concept of the Self frequently paraphrase Jesus: In order to find one's real Self, one must give up his lesser selves. Why is there this fight between the fragmented selves and the real Self? It is because of the *law of karma*, the law of cause and effect.

The *law of karma* expresses itself both through heredity and through personal choice. The latter kind of *karma* is known as *acquired karma*. Heredity conditions the setting for one's actions. The acquired habit-patterns of childhood and youth condition the choices of maturity. To the extent that one's actions are strictly thought-less, or habitual, the person loses

[1] XVI.1-5.
[2] II.41.

some of his margin of freedom. The cause-and-effect realm submerges the real Self. The person becomes less able to respond creatively to new situations that emerge. He becomes less aware. *Karma* thus binds man to a fragment of himself, or to a shadow-self. Habits once allowed a hold tend to maintain their hold. The not-self or the forces of instinct take over and dominate the real Self. In the figure of the *Katha Upanishad*, the horses (the senses) get the reins (the mind) in their teeth and run away with the chariot (the psychophysical organism), and ignore the charioteer. The problem is, how does the charioteer get back into control? If one's energies are dissipated in the pursuit of prostituted values, how does one become unified?

One of the first reactions which a person has when he sees that he has been living thoughtlessly has already been referred to—he tries to pull out of the struggle. But there is no exit in that direction. Lord Krishna says to Arjuna, 'If indulging in self-conceit, thou thinkest "I will not fight", vain is this thy resolve. Nature will compel thee.' [1] Man may refuse to accept the ambiguity of his predicament, but he is not thereby released from his ambiguity. Like Pilate, one may try to reject the problem of choosing, yet one's total being is choosing.

As a matter of fact, the person's dilemma is worsened by the refusal to meet the enemy on open ground. The forces which a man refuses to meet at the level of open-eyed consciousness burrow underground, becoming subterranean compulsions driving him to further distractedness. In the words of Krishna to Arjuna, 'That which through delusion thou wishest not to do . . . that thou shalt do even against

[1] XVIII.59.

thy will, fettered by thy own acts born of thy nature.' [1] To refuse to achieve genuine Self-knowledge is actually to choose further involvement.

The real Self must choose to know itself. To 'choose' flight is not a choice but a blind compulsion which, like a parasitical growth, derives whatever force it has from the real Self which it is trying to ignore. Before choosing one must reflect; only then can Krishna, the charioteer and the real Self, take over. 'Fixing thy thoughts on Me', says Krishna, 'thou shalt, by My grace, cross over all difficulties; but if, from self-conceit, thou wilt not listen [to Me], thou shalt perish. . . . Reflect on it fully and do as thou choosest.' [2] True choices are made only when the person's inner eye is open. Reflection helps to open the eye of the understanding. In this way the real Self gains the victory over the shadow selves.

Indian thought has steadily avoided any attempt to explain the actuality of emotional or moral confusion in terms of a personal Devil or a cosmic principle of evil. It has steered clear of metaphysical dualism—the splitting of the universe at its very core into two opposing principles, one of light and the other of darkness. Its traditional interpretation of spiritual and moral blindness, found in the *Gita* and elsewhere, is today finding some parallel in Western psychological analysis.

According to the *Gita*, that which is evil in the personality is itself derivative from the good or the result of a distortion of the good. 'What is man's will and how shall he use it? Let him put forth its power to uncover the *Atman*, not hide the *Atman*. Man's will is the only friend of the *Atman*. His will

[1] XVIII.60. [2] XVIII.58, 63.

is also the *Atman's* enemy.' [1] The lower self is not to be destroyed but controlled by the will held steady in knowledge of *Brahman*.

In other words, the talents, energies and potentialities of any person can be utilized either in Self-fulfilling or in Self-frustrating ways. A highly gifted neurotic uses his energies and gifts to remove himself progressively further from his true nature. The sharper his intellect, the greater his capacity for rationalization and self-deception. His very gifts become his inner enemy, keeping him from Self-knowledge. In Oriental terms, until such a person becomes sick of his sickness, the real Self cannot assert itself effectively or become a real friend. However, the suffering associated with the spiritual sickness is a friend in disguise, a warning signal.

A person's confusion is also illustrated by his inability to seek the right kind of happiness. According to the *Gita*, happiness is of three kinds. The lowest quality of happiness is of the nature of the *tamas guna* (the strand in man's nature making for dullness and inertia). This kind of happiness deludes the person both at the beginning and at the end. Above that is the happiness afforded by the life of action (the *rajas guna*), arising from the contact of the senses with their objects. These sense pleasures are 'like nectar at first but like poison at the end' and ultimately prove disappointing to the maturing person. The third kind of happiness is of the nature of the *sattva guna*. This tranquil happiness arises from some genuine knowledge of the real Self, and while it is like poison at first, it is like nectar at the end.[2]

Each person must discover the qualitative differences be-

[1] VI.5-6 (Prabhavananda and Isherwood, *op. cit.*, pp. 80-1).
[2] XVIII.37-9.

tween the different levels. The life of action is superior to the life of inaction; so is the kind of happiness associated with it. But both should be transcended by the higher kind of happiness which is the by-product of Self-knowledge. Each individual has his own particular temperament (the result of the initial blending of the three *gunas*). Hence each person must follow his own nature and earn his own insight. 'Even the man of knowledge acts in accordance with his own nature. Beings follow their nature. What can repression accomplish?' [1] The effects of past actions and of one's fundamental nature must work themselves out. One should not ignore them nor repress them, but understand them. Freedom is conditioned by heredity and environment and by accumulated habit-patterns. Motives may be mixed and clouded; so are all motives. 'One should not give up work suited to one's nature . . . though it may be defective, for all enterprises are clouded by defects as fire by smoke.' There is no virtue in trying to be someone else. 'Better is one's own law though imperfectly carried out than the law of another carried out perfectly.' [2] Each man can only be himself.

Why is it so difficult for a person to discover what it means to be himself? The *Gita* follows the *Upanishads* in saying that it is because of *avidya*, lack of awareness. This lack of insight expresses itself in the symptoms of egocentrism. One is attached to 'the I, the me, and the mine'. The *Gita* describes such confused persons as people obsessed with innumerable cares. 'Bound by hundreds of ties of desires, given over to lust and anger, they strive to amass hoards of wealth, by unjust means, for the gratification of their desires.' They are very attached to themselves and claim to be self-made. 'This

[1] III.33. [2] XVIII.48; III.35.

today has been gained by me: this desire I shall attain; this is mine and this wealth also shall be mine in future. . . . I am the lord, I am successful, mighty and happy.' [1]

Looked at more objectively, the condition of such people is one of bewilderment and entanglement leading to a foul hell. The gateway to this hell is described by the *Gita* as threefold—lust, anger and greed.[2] These all arise from attempts to dominate the not-self. In seeking to dominate, man becomes a slave to that which he mistakenly seeks and is doomed to perpetual dissatisfaction. The source of the dissatisfaction lies less in the inadequacy of the objects than in the confused expectations of the subject. Man seeks to satisfy the basic need for Self-knowledge with objects that have no lasting value.

More specifically, that which keeps a person from 'being himself' is desire. Chapter III, verse 39, refers to the 'insatiable fire of desire'. It is pointed out that such craving has its roots in the mind as well as in the senses. It keeps a man from wisdom or insight. It restrains him from achieving victory over the strife of opposites. Peace is declared to be possible only to the man who acts free from longing without any sense of mineness or egotism. It is not possible for the man who hugs his desires to achieve such peace. He who allows his mind to run after the roving senses has his understanding carried away 'even as a wind carries away a ship on the waters'.[3] Through following distorted desires man cannot come to any genuine Self-knowledge. The anonymous Christian saying—'Nothing burns in hell save self-will'—might be appropriately phrased, 'Nothing burns in hell save displaced desires.'

[1] XVI.7-18; II.71. [2] XVI.21. [3] III.39, 40; VI.5; II.70, 67.

Thus the *Gita* closes off a second blind alley down which man tries to go when the battle seems unbearable. The flight from life is ruled out since inaction is impossible to man: 'No man can remain even for a moment without doing work (*karma*).' [1] The lust for life is ruled out since it is a distortion of man's real needs. Where, then, is the middle path?

A CALL TO DISINTERESTED ACTION

With both inaction and attached action ruled out, Arjuna has only one alternative left—to act with detachment, or disinterest. Only in non-egocentric action is there Self-fulfilment. In the complete union of inner life and outer calling man finds his true nature. The key passage in the *Gita* on disinterested action states, 'To action alone hast thou a right and never at all to its fruits; let not the fruits of action be thy motive; neither let there be in thee any attachment to action. . . . Pitiful are those who seek for the fruits (of their action).' [2]

To action alone hast thou a right. There are two distinct perils in concentrating upon the anticipated results of action. The first peril is a relatively external one: no finite creature can long ignore the operation of the factor of contingency, chance or fate. In Western terms there is no way to insure against the future so far as individuals are concerned. Insurance statistics may tell no lies, but neither do they tell any significant truths. Man proposes, the future disposes—such is life in a realm of contingency.

The second peril is even more acute. No man who postpones the search for meaning today in the expectation of buying it tomorrow is really living. Nor is he truly teachable.

[1] III.5. [2] II.47, 49.

Tomorrow never comes. Man lives only in the now-moment, never in the future-moment. Meanings can emerge only in the lived-through experiences of the present. Meanings unappropriated today can never be brought back tomorrow—by material rewards, the ministrations of religion or by other devices.

Fixation on the anticipated results of one's actions thus tends to separate the doer from the deed. On the other hand, when a person is able to give himself wholly to the action engaged in, the whole self is fulfilled. Compensatory activities are unnecessary, since the action is integral. When integral meanings are not found, distorted meanings are sought as a substitute, but they have no continuity. At best they ease pain. At worst they prevent a person from finding more of his real Self. In place of continuity of meaning, the individual settles for atomistic experiences that haunt with their unsatisfactoriness. It is like trying to string beads without thread.

DEVELOPING 'SKILL IN ACTION'

How does a person learn to act without egocentric attachment? In answering this question the *Gita* redefines *yoga* as 'skill in action' or art in living. Men who would identify spirituality with strict austerities or self-torture are severely censured by the *Gita*. Of such people Krishna comments, 'Those men, vain and conceited and impelled by the force of lust and passion, who perform violent austerities which are not ordained by the scriptures, being foolish, oppress the group of elements in their body and Me also dwelling in the body. Know these to be demoniac in their resolves.'

The extreme ascetic is not an artist. The *Gita* is quite

aware of the self-delusion from which the ascetic frequently suffers. 'He who restrains his organs of sense but continues in his mind to brood over the objects of sense . . . is said to be a hypocrite.' Such a person rejects the objects of sense while his taste for them remains. One should neither fight the senses nor the taste for the objects, for this is to bind oneself to them. The man of disciplined mind can move among the objects of sense free from attraction as well as aversion. Only he attains purity of spirit.[1]

The *Gita* is highly selective in what it draws from Patanjali's *Yoga Sutra*. One is advised to seek a quiet place where he can be free of anxieties. He does not necessarily leave the householder state. Wherever he is, his prime duty is to practise moderation in all things. '*Yoga* is not for him who eats too much or abstains too much from eating . . . who sleeps too much or keeps awake too much.' Skill in action means developing a discriminating mind.[2]

The *Gita's* 'science of the Self' is thus an exploratory process of discovering meanings that authenticate themselves. All other arts and sciences are to be subordinated to the search for worthful integration having a cosmic base. A skeptic may deny the validity of such experiences until he has explored for himself. Just as the experience of healthy digestion is qualitatively and indisputably different from the experience of indigestion, so is the experience of reintegration at the opposite pole from a split personality. He who learns how to free his actions from inner constrictions knows intuitively the meaning of Self-realization.

Such a person, according to the *Gita*, gains a great sense of freedom. He is no longer bothered with cravings, he is

[1] XVII.5-6; III.6; II.59, 70, 64.

[2] VI.16, 10, 19, 23.

poised in the midst of sorrow; he does not long after happiness, he is free from fear and rage. Just as a tortoise instantly draws in its limbs when threatened, the enlightened man withdraws his attention from objects or attitudes that tend to enslave him.[1] Actions which previously combined healthy motivation with egocentric striving now become spontaneous and free. One is at ease within himself. The sense organs do their appropriate work, and the mind does its work. The resulting peace of spirit is not disturbed by passing moods of defection. Outwardly active, such a person is inwardly calm. He is Self-possessed in a way that the distracted person can never be. Others begin to emulate his character.[2]

Everything the enlightened person does is an act of worship, for worship is a matter of non-egocentrism. 'He who does work for Me, he who looks upon Me as his goal, he who worships Me, free from attachment, who is free from enmity to all creatures, he goes to Me.' 'Whatever thou doest, whatever thou eatest, whatever thou offerest, whatever thou givest away, whatever austerities thou dost practise—do that as an offering to Me.' [3]

The capacity for this kind of worship is in every man. This liberated state (sometimes described also as *Brahmanirvana*—the beatitude of God) can be achieved here and now. He who enters into it receives a sensitized spirit and conscience. He works with a new sense of the interconnectedness of all society. The old prejudices fall away—whether of race, class or creed. 'The wise see the same in all—whether it be a brahmin endowed with learning and humility, or a cow

[1] IX.28; II.55, 56; VI.19; II.57.

[2] III.20, 21; V.31; III.42; XIV.22, 23; IV.20, 22, 41.

[3] XI.55; IX.27.

or a dog or an elephant or an outcaste.' Compassion becomes all-inclusive. 'He who sees with equality everything, in the image of his own self, whether in pleasure or in pain, he is considered a perfect yogi.' [1] The test of spirituality is the quality of one's relationship to everyone, both friend and foe. This is worship in its highest sense, according to the *Gita*. Personal devotion to Lord Krishna, the incarnation of God, is the vehicle offered to those who travel the path of dedicated work (*karma* and *bhakti yoga*).

KRISHNA'S INCARNATIONS

The *Gita* teaches that there have been many incarnations (*avatarana*, literally 'descents') of the divine in human form. The concept is related to several aspects of the earlier tradition of the Myth. The Supreme Self or Supreme Light (the Solar Deity of the mythology) 'descends' to be a light to those in darkness. Or again, as in the *Brahmanas*, after the sacrificer has emptied himself out in the burnt-offering and has thus discovered 'Who' he is, he returns to the world.[2]

The descent of Krishna into the finite world is closer to the mythological figure than to the ritualistic figure just mentioned. Krishna descends into the world not because of any need on his part, but because of the need of mankind. It is man, cut off temporarily from awareness of his real Selfhood, who needs to rediscover 'Who' he is. Krishna thus descends not because of any compulsion or external neces-

[1] V.24; III.20; V.18; VI.29; V.25, 18; VI.32; XIV.25.

[2] *Satapatha Brahmana* III.3.3.10; *Taittiriya Samhita* I.7.6.6, VII. 3.10.4; *Pancavimsa Brahmana* XVIII.10.10; *Aitareya Brahmana* IV.21. Cf. Coomaraswamy, *Hinduism and Buddhism*, pp. 23, 31.

sity, but in sport or 'play'.[1] The *Upanishads* teach that the relation of man's true Self to this transient world is 'like the dewdrop on the lotus leaf', touching it but not adhering to it.[2] The Self has 'descended' into the body or impinges upon it, but is not to be equated with it.

The Krishna of the *Gita* says, 'Whenever there is a decline of *dharma* (righteousness) and a rise of *adharma* (unrighteousness), I incarnate Myself.'[3] This incarnation takes place in an inscrutable way through *maya.*

An analogy drawn from Western psychology may be partially helpful here to the novice. The term *autocorrectivism* is used to describe the innate tendency of the human organism to correct out-of-balance tendencies. Painful neurotic symptoms, for example, seem to be evidence of nature's attempt to restore equilibrium in the psychophysical organism. This inbuilt gyroscope is not of man's construction or willing. Yet when *adharma* (dis-equilibrium) has proceeded too far, *dharma* (equilibrium) seeks to re-establish itself. . . . In the *Gita* this is projected on a cosmic scale. *Dharma* is basic to the structure of the entire cosmic process at its higher level. *Adharma* is its temporary deviation at the level of *maya,* where the world is understood only fragmentarily.

It is possible that the category of *maya* may not seem so baffling, at least at the psychological point of view, if this analogy is pushed further. When a distracted or emotionally sick person comes to a critical turning-point in his relationship, he is either precipitated into complete mental illness

[1] *Krida, lila.* The life of this finite world is a kind of divine 'play', in the sense that sunlight 'plays' on the waves of a lake. The concept of the 'sport' of Krishna is a popular part of Indian religious life, recorded in song and legend.

[2] *Chandogya Up.* 4.14.3; cf. *Mundaka Up.* 3.2.

[3] IV.7.

(where he cannot assume any responsibilities effectively), or he suddenly achieves new insight into his problem. Whence this new insight? What are its dynamic roots? Why does it lead the previously distraught person on into creative areas of experience hitherto unexplored or unrealized?

Modern psychologists would like to know the answers to questions like these. However, the mystery of the relationship between a fragmented or shadow self and the real Self has not yet been resolved or understood clearly. In Hindu thought, among other meanings, *maya* stands for the inscrutable process whence the redemptive forces spring. Those who desire to 'know' the process truly must give themselves to the experimental process with all their resources. It is not to be grasped from a spectator point of view, of that the Indian sages are quite sure.

The *Gita* makes clear, in any event, that the theology of incarnations can only be understood from within. The incarnation is not a mystery to be accepted 'on faith', or least of all 'on authority'. It is something to be discovered or uncovered. An incarnation that happened only 'once for all' would have no real value, from the Hindu standpoint. The incarnation stands for an eternally operating principle and is not dependent upon a localizable event in past history. This point of view, developed consistently, frees man from undue servitude to historical facts interpreted in a fixed way or by an institution claiming to preserve the 'correct' interpretation of those 'facts'.

ALL PATHS LEAD TO THE SUMMIT

The West has commonly been inclined to regard its religion as 'the only way' to salvation. All other pathways have been regarded either as false or as inferior ways to the summit. The *Gita* reflects the much deeper understanding of the Indian mind with reference to the unity of truth and the diversity of pathways. The *Gita* rejects the chosen people complex forthrightly. 'I am alike to all beings,' Krishna says to Arjuna. 'None is hateful nor dear to Me. But those who worship Me with devotion are in Me and I also in them.' The resources for release (*moksha*) are available to all without favouritism. Not all may use the cosmic resources equally, yet they are there to be appropriated.[1]

There is diversity of pathways, however, since each person is unique by virtue of heredity and environment. Each must find and follow his own path. Though the pathways vary indefinitely in detail, all of them lead to a common summit. 'In whatsoever way men approach Me,' states Krishna, 'even so do I reward them; for it is My path that men follow in all things.' [2] Here is the note of complete catholicity. The honest believer does not cling to map, symbols or creeds, for he knows that each is relative to his own place on the path.

If *all* pathways lead to the summit, even popular religion of the unreflective sort seems to receive a kind of blessing. Should there not be a premium upon discernment? Hinduism has been quite tolerant of popular religious practices, as many Western interpreters have stressed. The *Gita* is not intolerant regarding the forms of popular faith which intermingle with credulity; but it does not teach that such forms are to be preferred to higher forms. 'Man is of the nature of his faith: what his faith is, that, verily, he is.' 'Whatever form any devotee with faith wishes to worship, I make that

[1] IX.29, 32. [2] IV.11.

faith of his steady.' This passage might be taken as an example of overlooking the fact that a person's faith can be attached to the wrong kind of object, thus involving him in further emotional confusion. But the immediately following verse points out that the fruits of such worship are quite temporary. The worshippers of lesser forms of good may cling to their symbols, concepts, or objects of devotion; but they thus miss the supreme good for which they are designed.[1] Those who rejoice in the letter of the Vedic scriptures, who are intent on heaven and concerned with the details of religious rites, are undiscerning persons. 'As is the use of a pond in a place flooded with water everywhere, so is that of all the Vedas for the Brahmin who understands.' The popular forms of religion lead to confusion. 'When thy intelligence, which is bewildered by the Vedic texts, shall stand unshaken and stable in spirit, then shalt thou attain to insight (*yoga*).'[2]

The illumined person, however, must be quite understanding in his approach to the devotees of the popular cult. 'He should engage them in action, himself performing it with devotion.' The example carries its weight by contagion, not by coercion. Helping others to find the way to freedom is the highest form of service. 'There is none among men who does dearer service to Me than he,' says Krishna.[3]

The *Gita* is theistic in that Lord Krishna is thought of as a personal form of deity. But its theism is a pedagogical device or a pointer. He who does not need theistic language can move ahead without being criticized. Through lack of understanding, a person mistakes the form for the reality or the signpost for the objective. In popular forms of reli-

[1] XVII.3; VII.21, 23.
[2] II.42-3, 46, 52, 53.
[3] III.26; XVIII.67-9.

gious devotion God or the gods tend to be thought of as being 'out there'; they become objects in a world of objects. This is picture-thinking, necessary at certain levels of human development. All of life is a school, however. Everything in it —including pictorial concepts—are of value to the extent that they help each person find his true Self. To this end all non-egocentric action contributes.

These are some of the suggestive insights of the Hindu tradition as focused in the *Gita*. The best-known modern Indian examplar of the way of life indicated by the *Gita*—Mahatma Gandhi—died on January 30, 1948, at the hands of an assassin. Non-violence (*ahimsa*) for Gandhi included the practice of outgoing love. His own interpretation of the *Gita* stressed the fact that the battlefield, described in the opening chapter of the *Gita*, lay in the heart of each man. One must work for good ends, even fight for them in non-violent ways, but with no attachment to the expected results. Shortly before his death he said to an American interviewer, 'Renunciation of the fruits of action does not mean that there can be no fruits. Fruits are not forbidden. But no action must be undertaken for the sake of its fruits. This is what the *Gita* means.' [1]

As few leaders of the masses of men have done, Gandhi laboured selflessly to improve the lot of the common people while reminding them, by precept and example, that the life of the spirit was of more transcendent importance than the life of the body. His own career was an extended commentary on the *Bhagavad Gita*.

[1] Vincent Sheean, *Lead, Kindly Light* (Random House, N.Y., 1949), p. 185.

CHAPTER SIX
TEACHINGS OF EARLY BUDDHISM

'Happiness he who seeks may win if he practise the seeking.'

'The burdened earth is sprinkled by the rain,
The winds blow cool, the lightnings roam on high.
Eased and allayed the obsessions of the mind,
And in my heart the spirit's mastery.'

Psalms of the Buddhist Brethren.

BRAHMANISM AND BUDDHISM

There is an uninterrupted continuity of traditional teaching running through Brahmanical and Buddhist thought. This has frequently been obscured by Western interpreters, who have lifted certain elements out of their context and dealt with them in such a way as to show their own European predilections. It has been said that 'the more superficially one studies Buddhism, the more it seems to differ from the Brahmanism in which it originated; the more profound our study, the more difficult it becomes to distinguish Buddhism from Brahmanism, or to say in what respects, if any, Buddhism is really unorthodox.' In the earliest period, there is no evidence of fundamental doctrinal opposition between Brahmanism and Buddhism.[1] The Buddha himself is reported to have said, 'I have seen the

[1] Coomaraswamy, *Hinduism and Buddhism*, p. 45; *Buddha and the Gospel of Buddhism*, p. 198. Cf. Mrs. Rhys Davids, 'Relations Between Early Buddhism and Brahmanism', *Indian Historical Quarterly*, X, 1934, p. 282.

ancient Way, the Old Road that was taken by the formerly All-Awakened, and that is the path I follow.'[1]

One source of the apparent doctrinal opposition between Buddhism and Brahmanism arises from the fact that Buddhism was opposed to 'the Brahmans of the court'—men preoccupied with the outward show of the ritual, thriving on comfortable fees from their royal protectors, proud of the fact that they were 'Brahmans by birth'. The Buddha's low estimate of the hereditary Brahmans was not out of step with the *Upanishadic* criticism of the false priests who were not 'knowers of *Brahman*' (*Brahmavit*). The *Upanishadic* attitude toward the worldly-minded priests is expressed in a satirical passage of the *Chandogya*. A group of dogs come together for a meeting, under the leadership of a white dog. The dogs request food from a person who has withdrawn to a quiet spot in order to meditate. The white dog asks the other dogs to return in the morning. The following morning back comes a procession of dogs. Each dog clutches the tail of the preceding dog in his mouth, imitating one of the stately ceremonies wherein each priest held on to the gown of the priest preceding him in the processional. In unison the dogs recite the sacred word 'Om, Om! Let us eat. Om! Bring us food. Lord of food, bring hither food, bring it. Om!'[2] Apparently for many the priesthood had become a racket, properly subject to this kind of satire.

That masses of the people had been left uninstructed by the Brahman class is indicated by a passage from another writing. 'While at Uruvela Sakya [Gautama] called to mind

[1] *Samyutta Nikaya* II.106.

[2] *Chandogya Up.* 1.12.1-5. Cf. *Brihadaranyaka Up.* 2.4.6.; *Chandogya Up.* 5.3.10; *Katha Up.* 2.23; *Mundaka Up.* 1.2.4-7.

all the different forms of penances which people in his time were in the habit of submitting to and which they thought raised the mind above all carnality. "Here", he thought, "am I born among people who have no prospect of intellectual redemption, crowded by revealers of the truth, with diverse wishes, and at a time when their faculties are wriggling in the grasp of the crocodile of their carnal wants. Stupid men seek to purify their persons by diverse modes of austerity and penance, and inculcate the same. Some of them cannot make out their *mantras* [scriptural formulas]; some lick their hands; some are uncleanly; some have no *mantras*; some wander after different sources; some adore cows, deer, horses, hogs, monkeys or elephants. Seated at one place in silence with their legs bent under them, some attempt greatness. Some attempt to accomplish their penance by inhaling smoke or fire, by gazing at the sun, by performing the five fires, resting on one foot or with an arm perpetually uplifted or moving about on knees.' [1] It was a time of confused people and confusing religious practices.

Buddhism has sometimes been contrasted with Brahmanism because of the former's alleged *atheism*. This epithet derives both from Western liking for short-hand labels and from woeful ignorance of what Gautama was trying to say. 'In reality, Buddhism is no more "atheistical" than it is "theistic" or "pantheistic"; . . . it does not place itself at the point of view where these various terms have any meaning.' [2]

[1] *Lalitavistara*, quoted in Radhakrishnan, *Indian Philosophy*, vol. 1, pp. 355-6, footnote (slightly abbreviated). Cf. Coomaraswamy, *Hinduism and Buddhism*, p. 46.

[2] Rene Guenon as quoted in Marco Pallis, *Peaks and Lamas* (Knopf, N.Y., 1940), p. 177.

What is involved in this statement will become clearer in subsequent paragraphs. Buddhism is no more of a deviation from the traditional Indian doctrine on all fundamental matters than the *Upanishads*. If both movements have been called 'Reformations', it is only in the sense that the 'established church' had lost its savour. No new doctrines were formulated.

What is known about early Buddhism is derived primarily from the literature of the Pali canon known as the *Tripitaka*, or three collections. Pali is a literary dialect closely related to Sanskrit. Western students of Buddhism became acquainted with the Pali sources of the tradition before the Sanskrit and Chinese sources. Hence a certain bias arose in academic circles in favour of the interpretation of Buddhism found in the Pali texts.[1] The Pali *Tripitaka* consists of the *Vinaya Pitaka*, which deals with the monastic regimen, the *Sutta Pitaka* or the teaching collection, and the *Abhidhamma Pitaka*, which presents the more abstract side of the doctrine. In this chapter and the following one we shall be dealing with the teachings of the Pali canon. Many of the more involved questions of interpretation cannot be dealt with in detail here. Even so, the path is not always easy to follow. None other than the Buddha is reported to have said that the doctrine is 'hard to be understood by you who are of different views, another tolerance, other tastes, other allegiance and other training.' [2] Contemporary Westerners tend

[1] The Buddhism of the Pali scriptures is also known by its later name *Hinayana*, meaning the Narrow Way or Little Vehicle. This term seems to have been supplied by adherents of the Broad Way or Great Vehicle, *Mahayana*.

[2] *Digha Nikaya* III.40.

to be very much involved in the life of the city, the market-place, and the amusement hall. The Buddha, on the other hand, teaches that man must leave the market-place in order to understand the world for what it truly is.

GAUTAMA'S AWAKENING

It is a mistake to try to understand Buddhism through a study of 'the historical Gautama', for Buddhist teaching negates personality as ordinarily understood. Yet many Western students have written to praise him or to censure him.[1] The significant events, spiritually speaking, in Gautama's early life were the 'Four Signs'—an old man, a sick man, a corpse and a monk. An over-protective father who wanted his son to become a great earthly ruler (for Gautama was of the royal caste) had kept the young man from contact with old age, sickness and death. Tradition says that it was the gods (*devas*) who assumed the four forms to acquaint the Prince with the true facts about life. Thereupon Guatama announced his intention of leaving the householder state, and in spite of obstacles put in his path by his parent, he made his escape from the world of the palace.

For several years Gautama studied with Brahman teachers; the tradition says he became as proficient as they were, but he was still unsatisfied. One of these teachers was a man named Alara. Had Alara been a more capable exponent of the traditional teaching of Brahmanism, it is possible that Gau-

[1] One Christian scholar, desirous of showing the superiority of Jesus to the Buddha, says that while Jesus died a young man on the Cross because men refused to accept his teaching on love, Gautama died an old man because of overeating. R. E. Hume, *The World's Living Religions* (Scribners, N.Y., 1931), p. 81.

tama and also his followers would not have opposed so vigorously what they understood to be false Brahmanical doctrines. Coomaraswamy comments that the parting of Gautama and Alara was one of the greatest tragedies recorded in religious history.[1]

Gautama also practised extreme asceticism or penance (*tapas*—a Sanskrit word meaning heat, glow or torture). Such extreme asceticism seems to have been commonly regarded then as indispensable to achieving liberation. Gautama was so thorough that he carried it to the point of death. Perceiving the foolishness of it, Gautama decided to take food and ever afterward taught a moderate form of *tapas*, a teaching not at all out of harmony with the *Upanishads*, which insisted that through knowledge alone could *moksha* be realized.[2]

The tradition relates that after bathing in a river near by, Gautama ate some milk-rice offered to him by a young maiden, threw the golden bowl into the river and watched it float upstream—an omen of his imminent enlightenment. Five fellow-pilgrims who had been with him during the period of extreme fasting meantime left him because he had taken food. Gautama then sat down under a tree, determined not to rise until he had attained knowledge of the causation and cure of evil, suffering and mortality. This tree became famous as the 'Bo-tree'—'Tree of Awakening'.[3]

Before the night was over Gautama had become a Buddha, an 'awakened one', knowing the cycle of becoming for what

[1] Coomaraswamy, *Buddha and the Gospel of Buddhism*, pp. 198-9.

[2] *Ibid.*, p. 214.

[3] For traditional details, see Introduction to the Jataka I.68.5 in H. C. Warren, *Buddhism in Translations*, Harvard Oriental Series, vol. 3 (Cambridge, 1922), pp. 71 ff.

it was. In the joy of his new-found insight, he uttered his famous song of victory:

Seeking the builder of the house
I have run my course in the vortex
Of countless births, never escaping the hobble (of death);
Ill is repeated birth after birth!

Householder, art seen!
Never again shalt thou build me a house,
All of thy rigging is broken,
The peak of the roof is shattered:
Its aggregation passed away,
Mind has reached the destruction of cravings.[1]

The Buddha remained for some time in the vicinity of the Tree of Awakening, conquering all temptations, including his initial hesitation to teach others something of what he had realized. Thereupon he set out for the deer park in Benares, where he found his five former associates. To them he preached his first sermon, usually called 'The Turning of the Wheel of the Law'. This sermon provides as apt an entrance as any into an understanding of the Buddha's doctrine.

THE BUDDHA'S TEACHING ON DUHKHA

Looked at negatively, the Buddha's teaching is concerned with the nature and origin of suffering and disharmony. Viewed positively, it is concerned with the path to the highest wisdom, to *Nirvana*.[2] Actually, the teaching must be viewed as a whole. Otherwise a Western interpreter is inclined to claim that Buddhism is 'pessimistic', since life as ordinarily

[1] Introduction to the Jataka I.76.17, verses 278 and 279, in Warren, *op. cit.* The above translation is that of Coomaraswamy.

[2] For detailed treatment of the meaning of *Nirvana*, see the following chapter.

lived is not an end in itself. 'Human life is of supreme value to the Buddhist as the only condition from which the highest good can be reached. . . . But we have to recognize that the quality of life is very varied, and Buddhism is far from optimistic about any and every sort of life, the mere fact of existence. . . . The common life of the world, according to Gautama, is not worth living. . . . But on the other hand he puts forward a mode of life for higher men which he regards as well worth living, and claims that by this life the highest good is attainable, and in this conviction that "Paradise is still upon earth" he is anything but pessimistic.' [1] It has been well said that such words as optimism and pessimism have no meaning in an investigation of truth. 'Truth does not need to be comforting; if some have found it so, so much the better for them.' [2]

Looking at life steadily, Gautama tried to see it as it truly was. 'How is there laughter, how is there joy, as the world is always burning? Why do ye not seek a light, ye who are surrounded by darkness? This body is wasted, full of sickness and frail; this heap of corruption breaks to pieces. Life indeed ends in death.' [3] 'I only teach two things, O disciples: suffering (*duhkha*) and release from suffering.' Gautama sought to break down the problem of suffering into manageable form. The Four Noble Truths are a statement of the problem and its solution.

The First Noble Truth is that of the fact of suffering. 'Birth is suffering; decay is suffering; illness . . . death . . . presence of objects we hate . . . separation from objects we

[1] Coomaraswamy, *Buddha and the Gospel of Buddhism*, p. 176.
[2] Marco Pallis, *Peaks and Lamas*, p. 156.
[3] *Dhammapada* XI.146, 148.

love . . . not to obtain what we desire is suffering. Briefly, the five-fold clinging to existence is suffering.' [1] (The five-fold clinging refers to the conditions of individuality or the components of the empirical personality: body, feeling, perception, will and reason.)

Gautama was profoundly realistic in starting with the fact of suffering. It was a *given* which none could think of denying and it called for no act of faith or acquiescence in a secondary authority. Each man's experience could speak for itself here. Gautama's analysis of the nature of *duhkha* deserves careful study, for the evidence from the Buddhist scriptures indicates that he used general terms with great precision. Unfortunately there are numerous general terms in Pali that have no exact equivalent in English or any other Occidental language. *Duhkha* is one of those words.

Duhkha is derived from two words—*khan* and *duh*. *Khan* means *hole* or aperture. In the *Katha Upanishad* it is used of the 'apertures' of the body, designating the sense-organs which provide contact with the outer world.[2] *Duh* means *bad*, and when combined with *kham* means 'bad hole'. When applied to the chariot analogy of the *Upanishads*, it throws real light on the psychological dimension. 'If the central hole of a chariot was not properly made, the spokes could not be properly fitted, and in travelling, the chariot caused a jolt or jar. The traveller naturally experienced discomfort under the circumstances. So *duhkha* meaning a bad hole was transferred to mental discomfort. . . . *Duhkha*

[1] The Four Noble Truths are expounded in the *Digha Nikaya*, the *Majjhima Nikaya* and the *Anguttara Nikaya* of the *Sutta Pitaka*, as well as in the *Vinaya Pitaka*.

[2] *Katha Up*. 2.1.1; 2.2.1. See comment by Nikhilananda, *The Upanishads*, vol. 1, p. 169.

denotes a state in which the sense-organs are injured, or contaminated or become unsound. . . . Where there is disturbance of harmony there is *duhkha*.'[1]

Such an interpretation throws additional light on the First Noble Truth. *Duhkha*, interpreted as commotion, disharmony or unrest in general, is a characteristic of the entire phenomenal world. The psychological counterpart of this constant agitation or 'chafing' in the world of becoming is dis-ease, irritability, unrest and pain or suffering.

To the person who is all-too-conscious of his own painful states, the Buddha offers both consolation and admonition. The consolation has nothing to do with the promise of future compensation for present suffering, but consists in asking the individual to see 'his sorrow not as "his own" but as world sorrow, inseparable from life itself'—an inherent characteristic of finite existence.[2] The admonition is to learn to see things as they truly are, without the dubious benefit of sweet-smelling perfume.

The Second Noble Truth proceeds to the diagnosis of the problem. 'Now this is the Noble Truth as to the origin of *duhkha* (suffering, dis-ease). Verily it is the craving thirst (*tanha*) that causes the renewal of becomings, that is accompanied by sensual delights, and seeks satisfaction, now here, now there—that is to say, the craving for the gratification of the senses, or the craving for prosperity.'[3]

[1] Jaideva Singh, 'The Concept of Duhkha in Indian Philosophy', reprinted from the *Ganganatha Jha Research Institute Journal*, vol. 2, part 4, Aug. 1945, pp. 357-68; a paper read at the Indian Philosophical Congress, Lucknow, Dec. 1944.

[2] Coomaraswamy, *Buddha and the Gospel of Buddhism*, p. 148.

[3] *Ibid.*, p. 40 (Coomaraswamy's translation).

Suffering, then, arises from craving or attachment. But Gautama does not let the analysis stop there. Craving roots back in ignorance or unawareness. Man is ignorant both of the real nature of things and of himself. Ignoring his real nature, man identifies himself with *what he is not*. The cause of all 'wanting' or craving is ignorance 'for we "ignore" that the objects of our desire can never be possessed in any real sense of the word, ignore that even when we have got what we want, we still "want" to keep it and are "in want"'.[1]

This is a profound insight that involves two important Buddhist concepts: (1) the doctrine of *karma*, or the teaching on the relation between action and ignorance; (2) the other is the famous *anatta* (non-soul) doctrine.[2] The first problem will be discussed in the following chapter in connection with the Third Noble Truth. The second question—what Gautama taught regarding the real Self—will be treated here.

WHAT IS THE SELF (ATMAN)?

Most Western interpreters have made the mistake of claiming that the Buddha denied the reality of a real Self. Here, it is asserted, is one very specific place where it is impossible to trace continuity between Brahmanical and Buddhist teaching. Eastern scholars have pointed out that this lies in a confusion of translation and in the lack of recognition on the part of Western students of the two entirely different uses of the word *Atman*. *Atman* for the Buddhist stood for the soul or ego, belonging to the order of

[1] Coomaraswamy, *Hindusim and Buddhism*, p. 62.

[2] *Atta* is the Pali for the Sanskrit term *Atman*. The latter term will be used throughout the discussion of Buddhism as it was in the chapters on Hinduism.

finite phenomenal things. For the Brahmanical philosopher, *Atman* stood for that which was beyond all phenomenal existence and which could only be described as 'not so, not so' (*neti*, *neti*).

Gautama and his successors apparently directed their attacks only against a popular variety of Brahmanism. Gautama may have taken exception to the *Atman* terminology without really understanding its deeper significance. Coomaraswamy says there is nothing to show 'that the Buddhists ever really understood the pure doctrine of the *Atman*. . . . The attack which they led upon the idea of soul or self is directed against the conception of the eternity in time of an unchanging individuality; of the timeless spirit they do not speak, and yet they claim to have disposed of the theory of the *Atman*! In reality both sides were in agreement that the soul or ego . . . is complex and phenomenal, while of that which is "not so" we know nothing.' [1]

Gautama's approach to the problem of achieving insight was essentially clinical or experimental. All suffering was traceable to craving. From craving comes clinging. Because man craves something, he clings to it either in idea or in fact. Craving and clinging are thus conjoined like Siamese twins. Gautama noticed that most people were clinging to the idea of the *Atman* instead of searching out the roots of their own ignorance. But 'all that is, when clung to, falls

[1] The same holds true of the Buddhist attack upon the concept of *Brahman*. It was the popular conception of *Brahman* to which the Buddha took exception. Coomaraswamy, *Buddha and the Gospel of Buddhism*, p. 199. Cf. Rhys Davids, *Dialogues of the Buddha*, I, p. 298: 'The neuter *Brahman* is, so far as I am aware, entirely unknown in the *Nikayas*, and of course the Buddha's idea of *Brahma*, in the masculine, really differs widely from that of the *Upanishads*.'

short'. Even a theory or concept of the supreme Real could be a stumbling-block. 'It is not the time to discuss about fire for those who are actually in burning fire', Gautama taught. 'It is the time to escape from it.' [1]

The Buddha refused to speculate about the Self lest people cling even more tenaciously to their own *notions* of the Self. He who is clinging to life or his ideas about it, identifies himself with his individuality, the 'I'. The ego or personality is only a temporary manifestation, a changing appearance. One should negate the ego, not 'express' it. For such expression is thoughtless and leads to further distraction. The *Dhammapada* says that 'the thirst of a thoughtless man grows like a creeper; he runs from life to life, like a monkey seeking fruit in the tree. Whomsoever this fierce thirst overcomes, full of poison, in this world his sufferings increase like the abounding Birana grass.' [2]

There are many passages in the Buddhist scriptures which indicate that Gautama assumed the reality of a Self. 'There is an unborn, an unoriginated, an unmade, an uncompounded; were there not, O mendicants, there would be no escape from the world of the born, the originated, the made and the compounded.' [3] There is a story of how the Buddha, on the way from Benares, met a party of thirty young men who had been picnicking with their wives. One of the group, having no wife, had brought along a woman companion who had seized an opportune moment to run off with all the belongings of the others. The men were trying to locate the feminine thief. 'What now, young men, do you think?' asked the Buddha. 'Which were the better for you, to go tracking

[1] *Majjhima Nikaya*, I, p. 29. [2] *Ibid.*, 32; *Dhammapada*, 334, 335.
[3] *Udana* VIII.3.

the woman or to go tracking the Self?' [1] The men decided that seeking the Self was more important and were converted.

Other passages distinguish between the 'Great Self' (*mahatman*) and the 'little self' (*alpatman*), and between the 'Fair Self' and the 'foul self'. The *Dhammapada* comments, 'One's own self is indeed difficult to subdue. Self is the lord of self, who else could be the lord? With self well subdued, a man finds a lord such as few can find.' [2]

There is a higher Self through which one conquers the lower, fragmented self. Yet the Self cannot know 'what' it is, because it is 'no what'. All that one can safely say of anything that passes as the real Self is, 'That is not my Self'. This formula is used repeatedly when Gautama is analysing the nature of the embodied self or personality. The 'stream of consciousness' composed of its 'grasping aggregates' changes ceaselessly: the body, feelings, ideas, volitions are never fixed. 'Just as the one word "chariot" is but a mode of expression for axle, wheels, chariot-body, pole, and other constituent members, placed in a certain relation to each other, in exactly the same way the words "living entity" and "Ego" are but a mode of expression' for the joint activity of the personality. No wise person will identify a portion of his experience with himself and say, 'This is mine; this am I; this is my Self.' [3]

The Buddha could rightly reply to criticisms that he was 'unorthodox' on this matter: 'Naughtily, falsely and against

[1] *Vinaya* I.23 (*Mahavagga* I.14). Cf. Coomaraswamy, *Hinduism and Buddhism*, p. 55.

[2] *Anguttara Nikaya* I.57, 58, 149, 249; V.88; *Sutta Nipata* 778, 913; *Dhammapada* 159, 160.

[3] *Visuddhi-Magga*, ch. 28 (Warren, *op. cit.*, pp. 133-4); *Maha-Nidana Sutta* 256.21 of the *Digha Nikaya* (Warren, pp. 135 ff).

the facts am I charged with being a misleader and a teacher of the cutting off, destruction and non-entity of what really is.' [1] A passage in the *Digha Nikaya* can conclude this discussion of the Self. In his last instructions to his followers Gautama said, 'Be such as have the Self (*Atman*) as your lamp, Self as only refuge, the Law as lamp and only refuge.' [2]

To refuse to say of any passing experience, 'This is my Self', is not to say, 'There is no Self'. Man can learn from his experiences, transient though they are, for he can observe how the contingent factors operate. It is not fruitful to raise the question, 'Whose consciousness is this?' for the only practical question is 'How did this state of consciousness arise?' [3] Man's destiny is not to identify himself with partial experiences or partial interpretations. Man needs only to learn how to cross the turbulent stream of craving. Man cannot do this if he remains on the bank of the stream theorizing about the Self. Once in the stream he must swim, not cling. A barnacle gives up swimming and settles down for life; man is not made to be a barnacle.

GAUTAMA'S EXPLORATORY METHOD

Gautama's refusal to deal with the Self speculatively is typical of his radical exploratory method. He is no modern 'empiricist' reducing everything to the measurable. Nor is he a speculative philosopher seeking to solve problems in terms of logical categories or neatly constructed theories. Both the empiricist and the speculative philosopher call upon

[1] *Majjhima Nikaya* I.137.

[2] Unfortunately this passage is frequently mistranslated, 'Be ye lamps unto yourselves . . .' But the Pali has no plural. *Digha Nikaya* II.101 (Coomaraswamy's translation). Cf. *Samyutta Nikaya* III.143: 'Make the Self your refuge.'

[3] *Samyutta Nikaya* II.13, 61.

their followers to 'believe' either what they see (that is, measure) or say (ideas, concepts). Gautama is unfriendly to both such approaches to life. Because of the period in which he lived, he was especially opposed to those who had 'views' or closed systems of thought. He wanted each person to get *a point from which to view* the human scene in its proper perspective. No one could get the right point of view while clinging to views. Gautama's call was to rigorous exploration of the 'Way'. His was an appeal for concentrated effort of the will leading to actualization.

Honest exploration meant refusal to accept the neatly catalogued answers of the past as definitive. The forests of India at that time were apparently filled with persons lost in the jungle of speculations divorced from the dynamic roots of the life process. The Buddha sought to mark out a Middle Path—a razor's edge between rationalism gone sterile and dogmatic denial of the place of reason in the preliminary stages of exploration. For him, reason was to be used as a sharp tool for cutting away the undergrowth in one's own thinking, not for hacking at opponents. Sixty-two schools of philosophy were holding forth in Gautama's part of the world. He refused to be drawn into their bickerings. Man's true end was to achieve liberation from the bondage of the finite world. That could not be realized if one sold his soul for a mess of metaphysical pottage or name-and-fame in the schools. 'Happiness he who seeks may win *if he practise the seeking*.'

Gautama did not find it easy to keep each seeker in touch with the concrete aspects of the problem. Not all of his associates had an equally keen awareness of the dangers implicit in dealing with a human problem primarily on the level of abstract concepts. This is well illustrated by a story in the *Sutta-Nipata*. One day a certain teacher came to Gautama to instruct him in purity. True purity, Gautama was told, comes only from philosophy. Gautama's reply was typical—inward peace comes neither from philosophy nor from the absence of philosophical opinions. He who holds to a philosophical position is concerned with defending it. This leads to disputation with rival opinions which in turn leads to pride, arrogance and conceit. Actually, one should get to the place where he neither desires opinions nor their absence. The genuine sage is the man who has shaken off all 'systems' of philosophy. Having no position to defend, he has no special prejudice to plead.[1]

Furthermore, Gautama points out, thoughtfulness is not to be confused with that kind of reasoning which is the standard practice of the world of philosophers. The wise person will practise thoughtfulness in the sense of becoming aware. Awareness is not increased by speculation such as the worldling engages in. Too many people make the mistake of going from philosopher to philosopher, seeking final truths. (Had not Gautama himself gone through this phase in his pilgrimage?) Such people 'following their desires, do not break asunder their ties; they grasp, they let go like a monkey letting go the branch just after having caught hold of it'. Grasping one philosophical position after another, they wander about in the world annoying people. In contrast to the emotional and intellectual confusion of such people, the Buddhist sage does not cling to anything—'to what is seen, heard, or thought'.[2]

[1] *Sutta Nipata* IV.9.1-13; 8.1-11; 3.1-8; 5.1-8.

[2] *Ibid.* IV.4.4.; 9.13; 6.9; 12.1-7; 13.1-20; 14.5.

Gautama makes the same kind of comment when a certain person asks him whether the world is eternal or non-eternal, finite or infinite. Such a question was considered quite respectable in most of the best circles of that time. Gautama's reply cuts through to the core of the man's problem: 'The religious life does not depend on the dogma that the world is eternal; nor does the religious life depend on the dogma that the world is not eternal. Whether the dogma obtain that the world is eternal, or that the world is not eternal, there still remain birth, old age, death, sorrow, lamentation, misery, grief and despair, for the extinction of which in the present life I am prescribing.' Such theorizing is 'a jungle, a wilderness, a puppet-show, a writhing, and a fetter'. It does not lead in the direction of supreme wisdom. Hence Gautama refuses to spin out another theory for his questioner.

Another kind of question seems to have occurred rather frequently: Is the person who has achieved deliverance reborn? Such a question was more mundane than questions about the world's finitude or infinity. Apparently *Upanishadic* teaching on immortality had not shifted the ground very much for the average person who was still talking about deliverance in terms of the popular theories of rebirth and the after-lives. Postdated hedonism still had its appeal, and negatively the threat of postdated punishment in another life.

To face such a naïve question while recognizing the honesty of the questioner required patience and skill. Gautama points out that it is not correct to raise the question in that form at all. He appeals to the analogy of fire. A fire burns only so long as there is fuel. The fire becomes extinct when the fuel has been used up. It is pointless to ask where the fire has gone—east, west, north or south. It is equally pointless to ask *where* the saint has gone. The person who has been released from the ordinary forms and entanglements of sensory life is 'deep, unmeasurable, unfathomable, like the mighty ocean. To say that he is reborn would not fit the case. To say that he is both reborn and not reborn would not fit the case. To say that he is neither reborn nor not reborn would not fit the case.' [1]

In other words, blessedness or true joy cannot be verbalized. Cessation of craving is something that can only be experienced from within. It has no necessary connection with the next moment, the next year, or the next life. Being anxious about the morrow does not help to solve the problem today.

One of Gautama's chief criticisms of religion and the priestly system lies right at this point. Most religion arises out of fear; the priests exploit this fear, especially as people approach old age. Such people, sensing that the end of life is near, put more and more emphasis on the offering of sacrifices. What they are really seeking is a continuation of their present selves. They tremble at the thought of their end.[2] Man in his egocentricity clings to his ego. Conventional prayer and the entire priestly system thus minister to his ego and his anxiety. *Nirvana*, or blessedness, comes, however, only to those who are thoughtful or aware—who 'have nothing in view' and no special ego interests to plead. Since *Nirvana* can be achieved only through seeking to understand the causes of craving, it is a dangerous habit to pray to the

[1] *Majjhima Nikaya*, suttas 63, 72 (Warren, *op. cit.*, pp. 121-4, 125).

[2] *Sutta Nipata* V.4.1-6; 6.2; 7.2.

gods, to men, or to his teacher for a removal of the symptoms.

We have seen how Guatama, in the First Noble Truth, has stated the nature of existence in a world of becoming—an existence characterized by *duhkha*, suffering or dis-harmony. In the Second Noble Truth he points out that *duhkha* roots in craving or *tanha*, which in turn springs from ignorance (*avidya*). In the Third Noble Truth, Gautama points out that the condition of ignorance is not incurable. 'This is the Noble Truth of the cessation of suffering: (it ceases with) the complete cessation of this thirst (*tanha*)—a cessation which consists in the absence of every passion, with the abandoning of this thirst, with the doing away with it, with the deliverance from it, with the destruction of desire.' [1]

This is the Buddha's doctrine of hope, an affirmation that man can do something about his predicament. To see clearly the ramifications of this teaching, it is necessary to understand clearly the Buddhist doctrine of *karma* and its relation to what is usually called the 'Wheel of Existence'.

[1] Version of *Vinaya Pitaka*. Cf. *Samyutta Nikaya* 22.85.1-56.

CHAPTER SEVEN

ON FINDING THE WAY

'The fool is like a half-filled water-pot,
The wise is like a full pool.'

'To every man that is born, an axe is born in his mouth, by which the fool cuts himself, when speaking bad language.'

Sutta-Nipata.

If a man has stumbled blindly into quicksand, it is not enough that he should be made aware of his predicament or instructed to take the matter philosophically. Positive steps must be taken to effect his rescue from the quagmire. This is analogous to the human pilgrimage. He who refuses to do anything about his involvement in the world of flux and becoming after having discovered the real nature of the marshy ground on which he stands sinks even lower.

According to Gautama, man does not need to remain a slave to craving. He does not need to remain bound to the 'Wheel of Existence'. It is up to him to see to the roots and gain freedom.

THE WHEEL OF EXISTENCE [1]

In analysing the nature of the relationship between suffering and craving and ignorance, Gautama used the figure of the Wheel. The circle representing the wheel is said to have

[1] Prabhavananda points out that the image of the Wheel as applied to birth, death and rebirth appears for the first time in extant Hindu literature in the *Swetasvatara Upanishad* (*The Upanishads, Breath of the Eternal*, p. 188).

been first drawn by him in rice grains on the ground, and was one of his earliest lessons to his followers. The Wheel has twelve factors, all of them operative in the experience of the unenlightened person. This Wheel has sometimes been referred to by interpreters of Buddhism as 'the causal chain'. This is definitely misleading. For one thing, it implies that Gautama was trying to get back to a First Cause; as a matter of fact, Gautama taught that the Wheel was without known beginning. Neither did he mean to imply that some causal 'entity' passed over into an 'effect'. Gautama spoke of 'dependent origination' and was concerned with making clear the steps whereby a person tied up in the knots of egocentrism and blindness could begin to see that the present phase of his existence was not the whole chapter in the book of becoming.[1]

Bearing in mind Gautama's non-speculative concern, let us look at the Wheel more closely. While the twelve factors are interdependent, Gautama and the Buddhists customarily begin the exposition at Ignorance or Blindness (*avidya*).[2] Blindness is the result of the crystallizations of past actions performed in ignorance of the real nature of things. From this Blindness comes more blind activity, the 'urge to live'. (Many forces are at work here, prominent among them the force of *karma*.) These two, Blindness and 'urge to live', are called the Two Causes of the Past. The first stage in the present life is Subconscious Mind. On Subconscious Mind depends Name-and-Form (the psychophysical organism). On Name-and-Form depend the six organs of sense (the five senses of Western thought plus the mind). On the six organs

[1] Cf. *Visuddhi-Magga* 17, in Warren, *op. cit.*, pp. 168-70.

[2] The following exposition is indebted to J. Takakusu's *Essentials of Buddhist Philosophy*, ch. 3. The entire chapter is worth careful study.

of sense depends contact or touch. (In the life of the very young child it is the sense of touch that predominates. The child begins to come into contact with the outside world.) On contact depends perception or sensation (*vedana*).

Up to this point in the developmental process, the individual is being shaped almost entirely by the forces of the past—forces beyond his immediate control. But in the remaining stages, the individual begins to create causes on his own responsibility. Thirst or craving (*tanha*) begins to assert itself through the operation of sensation. *Tanha* produces attachment or clinging; and on this depends Becoming or Formation of Being (*bhava*). What one 'becomes', in other words, depends upon what one craves. Craving, clinging and becoming are all intimately conjoined. Together these constitute 'the Three Causes in the Present. While an individual is enjoying the effects of the past, he is forming the causes for the future. While the plum fruit is ripening on the tree, the core in the fruit is being formed. By the time the fruit is ripe and falls to the ground, the core too is ready to being forth a new tree of its own to bear more fruits in the future.' [1]

That is, out of present Becoming, the individual plants the seeds of future births and future deaths—with all the sorrow, lamentation, misery and grief that naturally fall between. Birth and Death—the last two factors in the Wheel—can be regarded as an abbreviated description of the lot of the person who is still caught, through Blindness, in the realm of craving and becoming.

All twelve of these factors are interdependent, but the Wheel turns because of the action of *karma*. An excellent

[1] Cf. J. Takakusu, *Essentials of Buddhist Philosophy* (Univ. of Hawaii, Honolulu, 1949), p. 30.

interpretation of *karma* as the agent which keeps the Wheel turning is given by Marco Pallis, in his *Peaks and Lamas*. As he points out in interpreting the Tibetan representation of the Wheel, there is nothing but ebb and flow or continual becoming. All beings—human, sub-human and super-human—are caught in that same flux. The realm of becoming is not exhausted in this life. There is continual passage from one state into the next, but no one of the participating elements remains exempt from modification. 'Man is but one of an indefinite number of states of Being. His earthly life is but one episode among many others.' Pallis prefers to substitute the term 'Round of Existence' for 'Wheel', since it is the contents which remain perpetually in agitation, a tangle of orbits entering at every moment into new permutations. He suggests that a whirlpool is perhaps the best simile of all. Every person is caught in the vortex, by virtue of *karma*.[1]

He distinguishes four kinds of *karma*—(1) cosmic, (2) localized, (3) racial and (4) personal. The first includes the sum total of effects of all the actions that have occurred throughout the universe. The second refers to the actions bound up with the conditions prevailing in any subdivision of the universe (on our Earth, for example). Racial *karma* refers to the united causes and effects definable as heredity. Personal *karma* refers to individual acts and thoughts. Each type of *karma* can be discussed separately, but man usually starts with the last-named since that is where he first begins to become 'awakened'.[2]

[1] M. Pallis, *Peaks and Lamas*, pp. 145-6.

[2] See the entire essay, 'The Round of Existence', in Pallis, *Peaks and Lamas*.

Western students of Buddhism have always found it difficult to conceive how *karma* can operate either in a continuous line or a 'cosmic field' without involving the transmigration of souls. Since the term *samsara* has usually been translated as 'transmigration', the confusion has been increased. As pointed out in an earlier chapter, *samsara* really means stream or constant flow—and is descriptive of all conditioned existence. It is only in popular thought, both Eastern and Western, that *samsara* has been interpreted animistically as involving the transmigration of individual souls.[1]

A little reflection reveals that a much deeper principle is involved in *samsara* than this popular animism. 'The ending of one life and the beginning of another, indeed, hardly differ in kind from the change that takes place when a boy becomes a man—that is also a transmigration, a wandering, a new becoming.' [2] It is the influence that passes over; it is the man's character that goes on, not the man himself, for 'he' has no permanence.

The Buddha was not interested in the popular, animistic idea of transmigration save as a symptom of the basic human tendency to *cling*. He used many similes to show that no *thing* or entity or 'soul' transmigrates from one life to another. The favoured simile was that of the flame of a candle. The unlit candle begins to burn when it is brought close enough to the lighted candle, but the flame has not 'passed

[1] Coomaraswamy points out that the ambiguity introduced because of the two levels of thought—one animistic, the other metaphysical—was not entirely avoided in typical Brahmanical circles. It was Sankara, the great Vedantist, who stressed the distinction between exoteric and esoteric knowledge and thus paved the way for greater clarification on the issue.

[2] Coomaraswamy, *Buddha and the Gospel of Buddhism*, p. 106.

over'. Coomaraswamy suggests an even more pertinent modern simile. A series of billiard balls lie in close contact on a table. When another ball is rolled against the last stationary ball, the moving ball stops dead and the foremost stationary ball moves on. 'Here precisely is Buddhist transmigration: the first moving ball does not pass over, it remains behind, it dies; but it is undeniably *the movement of that ball*, its momentum, its *karma*, and not any newly created movement, which is reborn in the foremost ball.'[1]

When the doctrine of *karma* (or action-influence) is combined with that of *samsara* (the stream of becoming), a familiar truth of life is underscored: the history of the individual does not begin at birth; furthermore, the individual is always in *process of becoming*. Western psychologists, sociologists and anthropologists will admit this within a limited frame of reference; yet, as Buddhists point out, there is no empirical evidence against the wider grounding of this theory of action-influence.

The Buddha distinguished between two kinds of personal *karma*—fruitful *karma* and barren *karma*. The former binds a man to his illusions of individuality, separateness and the finality of the finite world of his experience. The latter releases a man from his egocentricity and from his tendency to regard this world as the last word in his experience. Fruitful *karma* can be translated as compulsive or egocentred action. Barren *karma* is enlightened, non-egocentric or liberating action.[2]

There are three conditions under which fruitful *karma* is

[1] *Ibid.*, pp. 106-7. *Milindapanha* 71.16.

[2] Part of this distinction is conveyed in the Western distinction between compulsive action and released action.

produced—covetousness, hatred and infatuation.[1] Actions performed under such conditions inevitably ripen in some future day or state. Such actions arise from ignorance of one's real nature. They are controlled from the cellar regions of consciousness and conditioned by the past. Of such a person it is truly said that he has no 'Self-awareness'. He is controlled by drives, urges, tendencies which 'he' has thoughtlessly allowed to accumulate. Such a person is not free; he is bound to the past and to the eternal 'round of existence'. He may claim to possess 'free will', but he is driven by his cravings, which have been fed by his ignorance. Resentful or covetous actions do not 'transmigrate' from yesterday's resentful act, nor do they pass over to tomorrow. But such actions are fueled by the same dynamic factors (the flame of *tanha*) which have not been rooted out through thoughtful attention or a metaphysical insight that sees through the physical or psychophysical.[2]

All blind or attached action thus produces fruitful *karma*—influence or tendencies that will bind one even further. As one flame is lit from another, so action-influence is transmitted. The foolishness of claiming that it is consciousness which is transmitted from one life to the next is illustrated by the fact that consciousness does not even remain the same from one day to the next. *What* each individual remembers is also highly selective.[3]

Barren *karma*, on the other hand, is action which is produced free from covetousness, hatred and infatuation. Such action-influences are 'abandoned, uprooted, pulled out of

[1] *Anguttara Nikaya* III.33.1.
[2] *Visuddhi-Magga* 17, in Warren, *op. cit.*, p. 239.
[3] *Samyutta Nikaya* II.95.

the ground like a palmyra-tree, and become non-existent and not liable to spring up again in the future'. There are no painful residues in character resulting from actions springing out of non-hatred and non-covetousness. Such persons do not feel 'like fish in a stream nearly dried up'. They have been delivered from the dead baggage of the past and are on the road to freedom.[1]

Let us return for a moment to the figure of the Wheel or Round of Existence. It has been pointed out that the Round depends on *karma*. *Karma* is itself the product of craving (*tanha*).[2] Craving and clinging both depend upon ignorance or blindness which leads to aimless activity, or the blind desire to live. It cannot be cured by intensifying one's activity, or by redoubling his cravings. Such obstinate attempts 'are as futile as the babblings of those who would make War to end War, or cast out devils in the name of Beelzebub'.[3] Blind action is like the agitation in the activity of a whirlpool. So long as man does not realize knowledge (*vidya*) to overcome ignorance (*avidya*), he lives out his life

[1] *Sutta Nipata* IV.2.6; *Anguttara Nikaya* III.33.2.

[2] It may be noticed that I have avoided using the word *desire* as a translation for *tanha*. This is largely because of the confusion that ensues when one English word is used to describe the whole gamut of desires, from uncontrolled desire at one extreme (*tanha*) to the eager desire for truth (*dhamma-chhanda*) at the other. Mrs. Rhys Davids has pointed out that both Müller and Fausboll, in rendering into English the anthologies of the *Dhammapada* and *Sutta-Nipata*, translate 'no fewer than sixteen Pali words, which really mean sensuous, or vicious, or unregulated desire, by the one unqualified word "desire"'. Mrs. Rhys Davids, Article 'Desire', in *Encyclopedia of Religion and Ethics*, vol. 4, p. 668b. Cf. Irving Babbitt, *The Dhammapada* (Oxford Press, N.Y., London, 1936), pp. xi, 74. In the *Anguttara Nikaya* (I.229) the sincere student is encouraged to pursue the truth with eager active desire (*tibbachhanda*).

[3] Pallis, *op. cit.*, p. 149; Takakusu, *op. cit.*, p. 31.

as a cork tossed about by the waves. Knowledge of his true nature and of the nature of the world around him would mean a new goal and a new method.

Thus in the Round of Existence everything depends on ignorance or arises from it. 'As I have told you, O priests, the first beginning of ignorance cannot be discerned, nor can one say, "Before a given point of time there was no ignorance, it came into being afterwards." . . . But there is an occasion when ignorance may be said to be a primary cause . . . when it is made the starting-point of a discourse concerning the round of rebirth.'[1] Ignorance of one's nature is real, but not absolute; man can take the steps toward overcoming it.

THE CESSATION OF CRAVING

In one of his treatises Augustine wrote, 'As a mother is pregnant with unborn offspring, so is the world itself with the causes of unborn things.' [2] Gautama suggested that each person victimized by cravings should penetrate into 'the causes of unborn things'. Gautama was quite sure that a person could be delivered from his accumulated *karma*. He was not a fatalist. 'O priests, if anyone says that a man *must* reap according to his deeds, in that case there is no religious life, nor is any opportunity afforded for the entire extinction of misery. But if anyone says that the reward a man reaps accords with his deeds, in that case there is a religious life, and opportunity is afforded for the entire extinction of misery.[3]

As indicated earlier, the craving to which man is subject

[1] *Visuddhi-Magga* 17, in Warren, *op. cit.*, p. 171.

[2] Augustine, *De trin.* III.9.

[3] *Anguttara Nikaya* III.99.1.

because of his blindness expresses itself in his clinging tenaciously to his individuality and what he calls 'his'. The man who suffers from egoism boasts, '"These sons belong to me, and this wealth belongs to me."' 'With such thoughts a fool is tormented. He himself does not belong to himself; how much less sons and wealth.'[1] Or man identifies his 'consciousness' with the Real. Yet consciousness, like the raft on which one crosses a river, is a means of functioning and is not to be clung to when one has reached the farther shore.[2]

The blindness that leads to craving can only be overcome through certain disciplines, to be described shortly, and a persistent watchfulness. On happiness, for example, the *Digha Nikaya* quotes the Buddha as saying, 'Happiness I declare to be twofold, according as it is to be followed after or avoided. And the distinction I have affirmed in happiness is drawn on these grounds: When in following after happiness I have perceived that bad qualities developed and good qualities were diminished, then that kind of happiness is to be avoided. And when following after happiness I have perceived that bad qualities were diminished and good qualities developed, then such happiness is to be followed.'[3] To achieve this persistent quality of thoughtfulness, the homeless life is recommended in many portions of the early writings as being vastly more helpful. 'Full of hindrances is the household life, a path defiled by passion, free as air is the path of him who has renounced all worldly things. How difficult it is for the man who dwells at home to live the

[1] *Dhammapada* V.62. Cf. Radhakrishnan, *op. cit.*, p. 415.

[2] *Majjhima Nikaya* I.261. Cf. Coomaraswamy, *Hinduism and Buddhism*, p. 81, n. 249.

[3] *Digha Nikaya* XXI.3.

higher life in all its fulness, in all its purity, in all its bright perfection!' [1]

FOURTH NOBLE TRUTH: THE EIGHTFOLD PATH

The Fourth Truth describes the way to the overcoming of *duhkha* and the realizing of true knowledge. The 'Eightfold Path' is a middle way between extremes—severe asceticism and self-indulgence. Both thoughtless asceticism and self-indulgence cannot point the seeker to his true objective; to covet pleasures or their absence is to invite pain, 'even as water pours into a broken ship'.[2]

1. RIGHT VIEW

The first step can be taken only by the person who stops to take stock of himself and his viewpoint. He must learn to see reality for what it is. He must not accept the Noble Truths on the authority of the Buddha. He must look into his own experience and see the facts of suffering for what they are. He must discover the correlation between his misery and his cravings. He must seek to find his larger frame of reference. Without this attitude—'right view'—no further spiritual progress in the path can be expected.

2. RIGHT ASPIRATION OR RESOLUTION

Right aspiration means 'the resolve to renounce sensual pleasures, the resolve to have malice toward none, and the resolve to harm no living creature'. It includes the hope to live in love with all.[3] This emphasis upon will, or right effort, in Buddhism is fundamental. It gives the lie to the popular

[1] *Tevijja Sutta* (quoted in Coomaraswamy, *Buddha and the Gospel of Buddhism*, p. 131 n.). Cf. *Majjhima Nikaya*, 87th dialogue.

[2] *Sutta Nipata* IV.1.5.

[3] *Digha Nikaya* XXII.

Western charge that the doctrine of the law of *karma* implies a kind of mechanical predestination. Instead of eliminating responsibility, the law of *karma* 'merely asserts that the order of nature is not interrupted by miracles. . . . I must lie on the bed I have made. I cannot effect a miracle and abolish the bed at one blow; I must reap as "I" have sown, and the recognition of *this* fact I call *karma*." [1] Right effort will create another kind of bed, or to use a more appropriate figure, will point one down the path to ultimate release.

Right view and right resolution belong naturally together on the 'Path'. The pilgrim starts by analysing the nature of his bondage: Why this over-investment in a world in flux? One is fettered to the world through the operation of the senses and the mind, arising from ignorance. These fetters must not be broken through extreme asceticism or a headlong assault on the psychophysical organism. Rather, one must learn to see the world and the human predicament for what it is; then as a consequence of right view, one resolves to renounce the false values (intellectual or physical) which lead to further bondage. 'By cleaving to anything . . . thus does one come to be; by not cleaving to anything, thus does one not come to be. Not to seek for anything, O priests, is to be free; to seek for anything is not to be free.' [2]

Right resolution includes relinquishing all anxiety about bed and board. The aspirant practises taking all things evenly. There is no place for possessiveness in him. 'He who does not think, "this is mine" and "for others there is also something", he, not having egotism, does not grieve at having nothing.' If touched by illness, he does not wish for

[1] Coomaraswamy, *Buddha and the Gospel of Buddhism*, p. 107.

[2] *Samyutta Nikaya* XXII.35.1 ff.

existence elsewhere. The thoughtful person does not grasp after anything in all the world; to do so is to become stuck fast in the realm of death. 'What is before thee, lay that aside; let there be nothing behind thee; if thou wilt not grasp after what is in the middle, thou wilt wander calm.' [1] Such a person is free from anger, trembling or boasting. As he gains increasing insight, hatred, arrogance, hypocrisy and all other forms of clinging drop from him—like a mustard seed dropping from the point of a needle.

Since the streams of thoughtlessness flow in every direction, they can only be restrained by the dam of thoughtfulness. Each person must come to an understanding of this in himself. Thus, long before Martin Luther, Gautama promulgated the principle of the *priesthood of all believers*. In his day, many a Brahman priest boasted of his lineage as well as his knowledge of the Vedic laws. For Gautama, a Brahman was any person who lived thoughtfully. 'The thoughtless man, even if he can recite a large portion of the law but is not a doer of it, has no share in the priesthood but is like a cowherd counting the cows of others.' [2] Not by birth does one become a Brahman, but by deeds alone. The true priest has nothing to do with ceremonialism, ritual or traditional prayer. 'Neither abstinence, nor going naked, nor shaving the head, nor a rough garment, neither offerings to priests, nor sacrifices to the gods will cleanse a man who is not free from delusions.' That the Buddha was not lacking in a sense of humour on this point is illustrated when he says, 'If the mere wearing of the robe could banish greed, malice, etc., then,

[1] *Sutta Nipata* II.14.17; III.11.34; IV.16.16; V.13.4; IV.15.15.

[2] *Dhammapada* I.19; *Sutta Nipata* III.9.38; IV.10.4, 9-11; IV.14.2.4; III.2.12-14, 19; V.2.3-4.

as soon as a child was born, his friends and kinsfolk would make him wear the robe and would press him to wear it, saying: Come, thou favoured of fortune! Come, wear the robe; for by the mere wearing of it, the greedy will put from them their greed, the malicious their malice. . . .'[1]

3. RIGHT SPEECH, RIGHT BEHAVIOUR AND RIGHT LIVELIHOOD

He who has achieved right aspiration and has become a genuine seeker is led on to the life of action. Steps three, four and five in the Eightfold Path are an exposition of what constitutes right action. Right speech is defined simply as abstaining from falsehood, backbiting, harsh language and frivolous talk.[2] Right behaviour means to abstain from destroying life, taking what is not given, or slipping into any form of immorality. This was later codified into the five precepts: Not to kill, steal, lie, be unchaste, or drink intoxicants.

On the positive side, right behaviour means the practice of love or compassion. Gautama taught that 'hatred does not cease by hatred at any time: hatred ceases by love, this is an old rule'. Even as a mother at the risk of her own life watches over her child, so every one in the fellowship was instructed to cultivate a friendly mind towards all beings. The real test of compassion comes when the Buddhist brother is attacked, with fists, stones, cudgels, or swords. Even under these circumstances he is not to harbour enmity toward his abusers.[3]

[1] *Further Dialogues of the Buddha*, Part I, p. 200 (Humphrey Milford, London, 1926). Translated by Lord Chalmers (*Sacred Books of the Buddhists*, vol. 5).

[2] *Digha Nikaya*, sutta 22.

[3] *Dhammapada* I.5; *Sutta Nipata* I.8.7; *Further Dialogues of the Buddha*, Part I, p. 90.

Mutual helpfulness, generosity, works of mercy and taking the good news to others are all referred to many times in the writings of early Buddhism. The great Buddhist king Asoka, who reigned in the middle of the third century B.C., revealed the influence of this principle when he caused to be carved in his Pillar Edicts: 'Not superstitious rites, but kindness to servants and underlings, respect to those deserving respect, self-control coupled with kindness in dealing with living creatures, these and virtuous deeds of like nature are verily the rites that are everywhere to be performed.' [1]

Right livelihood, the fifth step in the path, means that a Buddhist must choose a calling which will not force him to do things injurious to other beings, human or subhuman, or to his own spiritual growth. Certain occupations are to be avoided, such as those of the brewer, the butcher, the slave-holder or slave-trader.

4. THE INNER DISCIPLINES

The last three steps of the path have to do primarily with interior disciplines. Right effort involves many things—the control of the passions, avoidance of evil thoughts, stimulation of right states of mind. In this all-important discipline there is apparently a 'right velocity' at which one should travel. This fine point of balance between undue striving and undue laxity might be symbolized by the tuning of a delicate stringed instrument. Tonicity is achieved through the process of first relaxing the string a trifle below the true vibration till one becomes aware of the a-tonicity; then the string is tightened just a trifle beyond the pure tone to make sure one

[1] Pillar Edict vii.

has sensed both extremes; lastly, the string is relaxed just that small amount necessary to produce a tone free of all foreign vibrations or overtones. This 'pure tone' has to be discovered (at the middle point or razor's edge) by empirical investigation. But by this process the ear knows the true tone without any doubt when it is reached.

Right mindfulness, or right thinking, means living thoughtfully. One must be observant of the body, of sensations and of the mind, but not dominated by them. One must come to see all physical or mental states, either pleasant or unpleasant, as transitory. Instead of viewing things through the distorted spectacles of craving, one must learn to see things as they are. This is the attitude of the disinterested scientist. Illusory notions about life fall away only when man persists in trying to see things *as they are*.[1]

Amusing tales grew up in the Buddhist tradition to illustrate something of the nature of right mindfulness. 'Reverend Sir, have you seen a woman pass this way?' a traveller is said to have asked a Buddhist monk. The monk replied, 'I cannot say whether it is a woman or a man that passed this way. This I know, that a set of bones is travelling this road.' [2]

Right mindfulness was to be practised throughout the entire day by the thoughtful monk, no matter what his duties. Right contemplation, the last step in the Eightfold Path, was a much more specialized type of discipline. Many of the specific techniques utilized by Buddhist students were taken over directly from the prevailing *yoga* disciplines.

The practiser of right contemplation starts at the reason-

[1] *Digha Nikaya*, sutta 22.

[2] *Visuddhi-Magga* 1.

ing level and seeks to go beyond reasoning and reflection, perception and non-perception, to a level characterized by tranquilization and intentness of thought. This 'silencing' process is carried on through various stages of absorption, with the intuitive element increasing as the emotional and logical-analytical elements decrease. Gautama once said to an intimate associate, 'I have been alone in rapture of thought . . . till I rose above perception of the world without, into an infinite space of cognition, and this again melted into nothing. . . . Insight came, and I discerned with the celestial vision the way of the world, the tendencies of men, and their coming to be, past, present, and yet to come.'

Since people are different in temperament, not all are expected to meditate upon the same objects or concepts. At least forty different modes of training the heart and the mind are referred to in early Buddhist writings. Some of these were meditations on 'foul things' and were prescribed only for those who put too much emphasis on physical beauty. To help them become aware of the fact that even the most beautiful body is subject to decay, such persons were asked to contemplate human bones or half-decayed corpses.[1]

Other contemplations were prescribed for all of the brothers as a part of the daily 'work'. The first meditations were of an ethical character and were known as the 'Four Illimitable Sublime Moods'—loving-kindness, compassion, sympathy, and impartiality. One was to practise daily radiating compassion (*karuna*) in all directions, toward all

[1] *Ibid.* 3 (cf. Warren, *op. cit.*, p. 292); Coomaraswamy, *Buddha and the Gospel of Buddhism*, p. 144.

creatures. Coomaraswamy illustrates *karuna* from Walt Whitman:

> *I do not ask the wounded person how he feels, I*
> *myself become the wounded person,*
> *My hurts turn livid upon me as I lean on a cane and observe.*[1]

The true purpose of the Four Sublime Moods is to overcome any latent tendencies to ill-temper or resentment. But it is emphasized that the overcoming of resentment alone does not lead to *Nirvana*. To realize this one must have moved beyond both bad and good states of mind.[2]

A more advanced group of meditations consists of the *Jhanas*, which are disciplines of attention and abstraction designed to deliver the seeker from self-thinking and to lead him to know things as they are. This is literally dis-interested contemplation, for one is no longer 'interested' in the 'I'. Buddhist literature seeks to describe to some degree the nature of these various levels of contemplation, but they make little or no sense to the spectator or novice. One must pursue the path for himself, under skilled guidance, to discover their spiritual meaning. He who persists, realizes the supreme good—*Nirvana*.[3]

NIRVANA

What *moksha* is to the adherent of Brahmanism, *Nirvana* is to the Buddhist. The literal meaning of Nirvana is 'dying

[1] Coomaraswamy, *op. cit.*, p. 143.

[2] While bad states of mind lead to rebirth under painful conditions, Buddhist teaching emphasizes that good states of mind lead to rebirth under favourable conditions (described as rebirth in the Brahma Heavens of Form). But neither constitutes that kind of knowledge which gives emancipation. *Ibid.*, p. 145.

[3] Cf. Warren, *op. cit.*, ch. 4, 'Meditation and Nirvana', for passages concerning these meditations.

out', or 'extinction' (as of a fire), 'a blowing out' or 'despiration'. The term is older than Buddhism, being used in the *Upanishads* for perfect Self-realization. As used by Gautama it has its stricter etymological sense of 'dying out'—the extinguishing of the fire of craving. Anuruddha interprets the word as meaning 'a "de-parture" from that craving which is called *vana*, lusting'.[1] Gautama stressed that if a person refused to feed the flame of *tanha*, the fire would go out for want of fuel.

It is clear, however, that *Nirvana* has two dimensions—the first ethical and psychological, the second metaphysical. Liberation from resentment, coveting, lusting constitutes the ethical factor in *Nirvana*. Expressed psychologically, it involves relinquishing all sense of the 'I'. The metaphysical dimension refers to the cessation of Becoming and of ignorance. This cessation of Becoming is the supreme goal sought; the extinction of craving is merely a stepping-stone to this.[2]

The Buddhist descriptions of the person who has gained release from individuality and realized *Nirvana* emphasize the sense of freedom and spontaneity, the feeling of coolness after a fever has died down, release from a prison, clarity of vision.[3] There is joy in the escape from *duhkha* (dis-harmony) and *tanha* (craving), from lust (*vana*) and Becoming (*samsara*). The poetical similes used by the Buddhist monks never suggest any violent rapture or overmastering emotion. This

[1] *Compendium of Philosophy* IV.14 (Pali Text Society Translation Series, vol. 2); Coomaraswamy, *Hinduism and Buddhism*, pp. 63-4; *Buddha and the Gospel of Buddhism*, p. 117.

[2] *Samyutta Nikaya* II.115; Takakusu, *op. cit.*, pp. 52 ff; Coomaraswamy, *Hinduism and Buddhism*, p. 64; *Buddha and the Gospel of Buddhism*, pp. vii, 117-18.

[3] *Further Dialogues of the Buddha*, part 1, pp. 194-7.

sense of freedom does not mean an immediate release from mortality. 'As the bee collects nectar and departs without injuring the flower or its colour or scent', so does the enlightened one dwell in his village. Having sensed the delusion of egoism and ambition, he lives without clinging—like water on a lotus leaf, like the wind not caught in a net.[1]

Having given up all things, all things become his in a new dimension. With appetites overcome, he is free even in the world. Gone is the old cramping sense of life; in its place is life in the open air. Gone is the feeling of depression; in its place is a feeling of tranquil joy. Whereas the careless pilgrim only scatters the dust of his passions more widely, the thoughtful pilgrim lives in complete possession of himself. Having cut out the love of self like an autumn lotus, one now travels the road of peace. Yet this road of peace is not the road of inertia or inaction. Gautama admonishes his friends, 'Like a well-trained horse when touched by the whip, be ye active and lively, and by faith, by virtue, by energy, by meditation, by discernment of the law you will overcome this great pain . . . perfect in knowledge and behaviour, and never forgetful.' [2] Such statements underscore the distinction between the lust for life and love of truth.

The writings of the Buddhists indicate that Gautama and others in the fellowship passed in and out of this highest rapture, or state of superconsciousness. This led to a distinction between *Nirvana* and *Parinirvana* (complete or final dying out), the latter being coincident with physical death. Gautama stood with the mystics of all traditions in emphasiz-

[1] *Sutta Nipata* I.3.22, 37; II.13.4.11; III.9.32; *Dhammapada* XXVI. 401.

[2] *Dhammapada* IV.49; V.62; VI.89; X.144; XV.197; XX.285; XXII. 313.

ing that *Nirvana* is accessible here and now; what lay beyond death he strictly refused to discuss as such a 'realization' was non-thinkable. '*Nirvana* is a final end and . . . a matter about which no further questions can be asked by those who are still on fire.' [1]

Since *Nirvana* has been so commonly misunderstood by Western interpreters, an additional comment is in order. Too often has it been rendered by the one word 'extinction'. Coomaraswamy is a much more competent guide in these matters: '*Nirvana*', he says, 'is a kind of death, but like every death a rebirth to something other than what had been.' He points out that the Buddha uses the word chiefly 'in connection with the "quenching" of the fires of passion, fault and delusion'.

This ethical psychological dimension of the term is easier for the Western mind to grasp than the metaphysical. To die to egocentrism and all of its disturbing symptoms is one thing; for the human organism suddenly to die or expire is something different. No person achieves deeper insights without dying to outworn ones. Knowledge or awareness always means death—death of all clinging to old forms, outmoded perspectives and ideas. An old chapter is closed, finished, 'extinguished' like a flame. To live at the highest involves 'practising dying daily', as various mystics have expressed it. The genuine scientist—like the true mystic—always stands on a frontier. Many people hesitate to explore near the frontiers of knowledge because of their liking for the lure of the old, the taste for antiquated things which is a kind of spiritual nostalgia. What is this but to become so-

[1] Coomaraswamy, *Hinduism and Buddhism*, p. 64; *Majjhima Nikaya* I.304; *Samyutta Nikaya* III.188.

journers on the land when men are called to be explorers of the frontiers? 'Promised Lands' are always traps for the thoughtless. He who has coveted milk and honey in his lean years tends to settle for material security in his more prosperous years. The Buddha would remind every man that this world is only an intermediate stage in the realm of becoming.

Hence the 'extinguishing' for which *Nirvana* stands has a metaphysical dimension as well as an ethical-psychological one. What is a present psychological experience regarded from the point of view of the temporal frame of reference is also an eternal (i.e. time-less) event involving liberation from *ignorance* and from the whole realm of becoming (*avidya* and *samsara*). Thus *Nirvana* must not be reduced to a state of the mind or of the 'psyche', for one must be liberated even from the 'psyche'. In one passage the Buddha says, 'I call him a Brahman indeed who has passed beyond attachment both to good and evil; one who is clean, to whom no dust attaches, a-pathetic.' [1] There must be a total 'un-selfness'; this combines the two ideas of 'being perfected' and 'dying'.[2] One is beyond good and evil, selfishness and unselfishness; for such terms have real meaning only in the context of a

[1] *Dhammapada* 412 (Coomaraswamy's translation).

[2] Coomaraswamy points out that the denotation is that of quenching fire or passion, but the connotation is that of Greek *teleō* and *teleutaō*—to be perfected, to die. 'All these meanings can be resumed in the one English word "finish"; the finished product is no longer in the making, no longer *becoming* what it ought to be; in the same way the finished being, the perfected man, has done with all becoming; the final dissolution of the body cannot affect him, however affecting it may be to others, themselves imperfect, unfinished. *Nirvana* is a final end, and like *Brahma*, a matter about which no further questions can be asked by those who are still on fire.' Coomaraswamy, *Hinduism and Buddhism*, p. 64.

life lived dualistically. Conscious of two contradictory impulses within, man fights his 'selfishness' by marshalling forces of 'unselfishness'. However, he who has died to self-centredness, has died to 'others' as well as to 'self'. '. . . If the "dead man" seems to be "unselfish", this will not be the result of altruistic motives, but accidentally, and because he is literally un-self-ish.' [1]

Ethical disciplines and psychological insights are like the raft by means of which one crosses a river. They are means to an end which cannot be described in terms of the steps one took in approaching that end. Hence Gautama wisely refused to debate what 'happened' to the person who realized *Nirvana*. *Nirvana* was not something to be debated but to be realized by those willing to undertake the experiment in following the prescribed techniques. No definition could help the man who had not been delivered from his need to cling. No interpretation would be necessary for the man who had discovered it for himself. The serious pilgrim was promised release from *duhkha* (dis-harmony) and *avidya* (un-awareness). But the Buddha never encouraged anyone to eliminate the suffering or dis-harmony; he asked him to go to the roots. To know to the roots is to get at the causes. *To know to the roots brings freedom.*

[1] Coomaraswamy, *Hinduism and Buddhism*, p. 17.

CHAPTER EIGHT

OTHERS SEEK THE WAY OF THE BUDDHA

'I would be a protector of the unprotected, a guide to wayfarers . . . a bridge for them who seek the further Shore; a lamp for them who need a lamp, a bed for them who need a bed, a slave for all beings who need a slave.'—SANTIDEVA.

THE divine powers that most people in their unreflective moments believe in are the creation of man's own needs. Popular religion, or the religion of the masses, moves primarily on the level of petitional prayer. For such people their wants are their gods, as Meister Eckhart put it. They 'want to see God with their eyes as they see a cow and to love him as they love their cow—they love their cow for the milk and cheese and profit it makes them'.[1]

This kind of 'religion' was widespread in India when Gautama was teaching. He avoided the emotionally-freighted symbols of such beliefs and practices as a snare and a delusion. Any peace of mind earned in such a fashion he regarded as both precarious and spurious. Each man must go into the depths for himself and explore. Each must be unwilling to be bought off with the enticements of an earth-bound religion which regards the gods as cows waiting to be milked. To Gautama, popular religion was one symptom

[1] R. Blakney, *Meister Eckhart: A Modern Translation* (Harper, N.Y., 1941), p. 241.

indicating how sick man was. Hence he proposed no such short-cut to *Nirvana*.

The kind of approach advocated by the Buddha put a premium on the educational process and on actual experimentation, including the various stages of contemplation. The self-authenticating insights emerge in the exploration; *Nirvana* must be inwardly appropriated. Teachers are helpful only if they themselves have realized the higher stages of consciousness.

Gautama's emphasis on the importance of knowledge did not rule out other values. One was to be un-worldly, not attached to this finite realm of becoming; that one was not supposed to be 'other-worldly', however, is indicated by the stress he placed on compassion. Only if a person had discovered the meaning of enlightenment was he capable of being truly compassionate. This latter point deserves comment, for many interpreters of the Buddha's teaching insist that there were two conflicting strands in his thought. The disciple was first urged to become composed in mind, seeing all things evenly or objectively. Then he was instructed to display love and compassion for all fellow-creatures. How the two attitudes could be cultivated in one and the same person has been the problem for the interpreters. 'To be "composed in mind" yet at the same time to be "shaken with compassion" is a difficult performance', Pratt comments. He cites the first *Jataka* story, according to which Gautama, in a previous birth, came across a starving tiger. The tale records that Gautama, 'though composed in mind, was shaken with compassion by the sufferings of his fellow-creatures as Mt. Meru is by an earthquake'.[1]

[1] J. B. Pratt, *Pilgrimage of Buddhism* (Macmillan, N.Y.), p. 93.

Are composure and compassion irreconcilable? Gautama taught that one was to cultivate composure of mind in order to overcome craving. He who achieved release from his addiction to the world of transitoriness gained a new sense of freedom which expressed itself in terms of joy, sympathy, love and compassion. The Buddha's compassion, then, was the product of genuine release from craving and ignorance. Modern psychology suggests something which points in this direction. He who is subject to neurotic attachments cannot be truly compassionate. His sympathy or love proceeds from distorted ego-needs. He loves possessively, not because of a real concern for the object of his love. He may be generous with 'sympathy' only because he feels the need of it so desperately himself. On the other hand, the mature person gives sympathy objectively; he does not minister subtly to his own distorted needs through the other person. A mother who is objective about her own emotional needs loves her child responsibly rather than possessively.

According to the Buddhist analysis, composure of mind is only the prelude to the compassionate heart. Gautama's life was not lived on two levels—his theory pointing in the direction of self-centredness and his practice in the direction of altruism. His theory served the basic purpose of clearing the path for a more humane practice. His own life was remarkably consistent and balanced, especially in a time when spirituality was often confused with complete denial of the life of desire. Spirituality, the Buddha discerned, was not to be found in negation in and for itself. It was to be found in terms of what one affirmed and how he affirmed it. If many of Gautama's followers became life-negating, instead of ego- and world-negating, it was because of an inability to follow through on the implications of his analysis of the nature and roots of craving.

RISE OF DIVERGENT INTERPRETATIONS

In the century following upon the death of Gautama, all of the religious movements of India displayed pronounced popularizing tendencies. It was a period of religious revival, but at a level adapted to the confused emotional life of the masses. Men demanded idealized objects of devotion —personal gods or saviours to whom they could turn, or more vivid symbols to help them in their search for release.

This widespread flight into the derivative forms of the religious life influenced the Buddhist tradition also. Gautama had put the emphasis on individual exploration. Within a few years after his death, initiates into the order were reciting, 'I take my refuge in the Buddha, I take my refuge in the *Dhamma*, I take my refuge in the *Sangha*.' [1] Gautama had asked his friends to take his words experimentally and not uncritically.[2] Many of his followers began to make a cult of him and of his teachings. The *Sangha* originally was simply the fellowship of seekers gathered around Gautama. It became a church and a missionary society. The strong personal loyalty felt by the early disciples was passed on to succeeding generations of followers. Eventually Gautama was transformed into a god.

During the early stages of this development, Buddhist figures or statues were introduced into the monasteries. The

[1] *Dhamma*, norm or teachings (in this particular context). *Sangha*, the Order, or congregation.

[2] *Majjhima Nikaya* XXXVIII.

room in which they were placed was usually the great meeting-room. Thus the room gradually became a temple. From such simple beginnings as these came the later, elaborate temples in which worshippers were to bow down before life-size statues of the Buddha. The relics of Gautama were also being reverenced shortly after his decease. Pilgrimages came into vogue. The faithful journeyed to his birthplace, to the site of his enlightenment, to the place where he had preached his first sermon, and to the place of his death.

In the two centuries subsequent to the death of the Buddha a great many disputes arose between divergent Buddhist sects, each of which tended to assume that it stood the closest to the true doctrine. The Theravadins (or the 'Elders') used texts written in Pali and they claimed to be the 'original' Buddhists. They emphasized the ideal of the monk who 'wandered lone as the rhinoceros'. They stressed the strict observance of the rules of the monastic order, leading in some cases to a kind of monastic legalism.[1] This development subsequently came to be nicknamed the *Hinayana* ('Little Vehicle') by adherents of another wing who appropriated the term *Mahayana* ('Great Vehicle').

Starting in India, the *Mahayana* form of Buddhism spread to China, Japan and Tibet, and proved remarkably adapted to the temperament of the Far Eastern peoples. In place of the Pali scriptures, *Mahayana* used Sanskrit texts which were translated into Chinese and Japanese.[2] It has been the stand-

[1] Cf. Ryukan Kimura, *A Historical Study of the Terms Hinayana and Mahayana and the Origin of Mahayana Buddhism* (Univ. of Calcutta, Calcutta, 1927).

[2] *Ibid.*

ing criticism of *Hinayana* Buddhists against the *Mahayanists* that the latter do not have the authentic teaching of the Buddha. Many scholars, both Buddhist and non-Buddhist, admit that the seeds of the developed *Mahayana* teachings are to be found in the earliest reported teachings of Gautama. *Mahayanists* themselves admit that their scriptures did not come into existence during the Buddha's lifetime, but they point out (and rightly) that the same is true of the Pali canon of *Hinayana* Buddhism.

The Buddhist doctrine very obviously underwent growth in all of its schools. One of the fundamental teachings of Buddha had been that of *anicca* (transiency). Interpretations of the doctrine were bound to grow since they too were subject to *anicca*. The *Hinayana* schools stressed salvation through knowledge and the monastic order. The *Mahayana* schools were to stress salvation through knowledge expressing itself in terms of faith and love. This meant much less emphasis on the monastery and more emphasis on dedicated work in the world of suffering beings. The ideal of the *Theravadins* was definitely limited, designed only for those who had left their spiritual childhood far behind, whereas *Mahayana* was adapted to the varying needs of the 'children of the Buddha'.[1]

The greater catholicity of *Mahayana* is indicated in the doctrine of *upaya* (expediency, or convenient means). Various skilful means, stratagems, or expedient devices are recommended to help different people come to intuitive realization. The goal—enlightenment—is one, but the 'means' to that goal are many. In *Mahayana* circles the doctrine of *upaya* is practically synonymous with love. Any and all means that

[1] Coomaraswamy, *Buddha and the Gospel of Buddhism*, pp. 226-9.

relieve beings of blindness and misery, leading them to enlightenment, are truly expedient.[1] This brings us to what Pallis has called the presiding idea in *Mahayana* Buddhism—*Bodhisattvahood.*

LOVE AND THE IDEAL OF THE BODHISATTVA

The term *Bodhisattva* means one whose nature consists of insight.[2] Pallis describes the *Bodhisattva* as an awakened being 'who, though under no further constraint by that Law of Causality which he has transcended, yet freely continues to espouse the vicissitudes of the Round of Existence by virtue of his Self-identification with all the creatures still involved in egocentric delusion and consequent suffering'.[3] He does not do this out of any sentimental 'altruism', for having gone beyond the sense of an 'I', he is also beyond the concept of 'other'. For him all of the old dualisms—between good and bad, bondage and deliverance (*samsara* and *Nirvana*), 'I' and 'thou'—have dissolved. Living in the world of becoming with its correlated suffering, still he is aware of the changeless joy of *Nirvana*. Having identified his 'Self' with the 'Self' in all other beings, he lives a compassionate life.

The *Bodhisattva* ideal grew up around the example of Gautama, who, after his enlightenment, spent the remainder of his life teaching his friends how they might realize the same kind of experience. Out of compassion the Buddha chose to help others. What Gautama did was identical with what all of the other Buddhas who had appeared in the past

[1] Beatrice L. Suzuki, *Mahayana Buddhism, A Brief Outline* (Marlowe, London, 1948), p. 59.

[2] *Bodhi-sattva*, wisdom-being.

[3] M. Pallis, *Peaks and Lamas*, second ed. (Knopf, N.Y., 1949), p. 303.

had done—they had dedicated themselves to the welfare of others before consenting to become Buddhas.[1]

Of the many Buddhas revered in Chinese and Japanese circles, *Amitabha* or Measureless Light (*Amida* in Japan) is one of the most popular. His importance arises from the tradition that he was once a monk who, infinite ages ago, made forty-six vows out of love for his fellow beings. He desired to devote all of his wisdom or merits to the saving of others. The eighteenth vow is the most important:

'O Bhagavat, if those beings who have directed their thought towards the highest perfect knowledge in other worlds and who, having heard my name, when I have attained *Bodhi* (knowledge), have meditated on me with serene thoughts; if at the moment of their death, having approached them, I should not stand before them . . . so that their thoughts should not be troubled, then may I not attain the highest, perfect knowledge.' [2]

Through the years *Amitabha* fulfilled these vows and built up a tremendous Treasury of Merit. This merit is sometimes referred to as 'the Ship of the Vow'. It is comparable to the teaching of some of the early Christian church fathers, that the Church is 'the Ark of Salvation'. 'The Ship of the Vow' can easily carry the sins of the unenlightened ones, though otherwise these sins are as heavy as stones and would sink to the bottom of the ocean. Through his merits *Amitabha* established a Pure Land or Western Paradise where he can

[1] Even the scriptures of the *Hinayana* schools did not teach that Gautama was the only Buddha or Enlightened One. At least seven Buddhas were recognized at an early period. As the Buddhist imagination continued to develop this idea, the number of Buddhas increased till eventually hundreds of millions were recognized.

[2] B. L. Suzuki, *op. cit.*, pp. 54-5.

receive all those who place themselves on his ship, to be borne across the ocean of *samsara* (the world of suffering and frustration). *Amitabha* is the embodiment of perfect mercy and wisdom. Whoever meditates upon him with devotion is assured of entering into Paradise through receiving a portion of the Saviour's superabundant merit.[1]

This *parivarta* doctrine (the turning over of merit to the advantage of others) underscores the *Mahayana* sense of the interdependence of all life. Early Buddhism had emphasized the separateness of lives in so far as the law of *karma* was thought of as working in essentially singular (though parallel) lines. *Mahayana* Buddhism teaches that the whole creation shares a common *karma* (both racial and cosmic). In this view the operation of the law of *karma* would have to be symbolized by an intricately complex net or tangled skein. Every individual contributes to this common *karma* for good or for ill. In late Buddhism 'whoever accomplishes a good deed, such as a work of charity or a pilgrimage, adds the prayer that the merit may be shared by all sentient beings'.[2]

The *Bodhisattva* ideal has been beautifully expressed in the writings of a seventh-century poet, Santideva.

In reward for all this righteousness that I have won
by my works, I would fain become a soother of all the
sorrows of all creatures.

May I be a balm to the sick, their healer and servitor,
until sickness come never again.

[1] See story about him in *S.B.E.*, vol. 49, part 2, p. 7. Cf. Suzuki, *op. cit.*, pp. 48-51; James Troup's paper on the Shin sect, read to the Asiatic Society of Japan, Oct. 1855, and quoted in B. H. Streeter, *The Buddha and the Christ* (Macmillan, N.Y., 1933), pp. 90-1.

[2] Coomaraswamy, *op. cit.*, p. 231.

May I quench with rains of food and drink the anguish of hunger and thirst. May I be, in the famine at the ages' end, their drink and meat.

May I become an unfailing store for the poor, and serve them with manifold things for their need.

My own being and my pleasures, all my righteousness in the past, present or future I surrender indefinitely, that all creatures may win to their end.

The Stillness lies in surrender of all things, and my spirit is fain for the Stillness. If I must surrender all, it is best to give it for fellow-creatures.

I yield myself to all living things to deal with me as they list; they may smite or revile me for ever, bestrew me with dust, play with my body, laugh and wanton; I have given them my body, why shall I care?

May all who slander me, or do me hurt, or jeer at me, gain a share in the Enlightenment.

I would be a protector of the unprotected, a guide to wayfarers, a ship, a dyke, and a bridge for them who seek the further Shore; a lamp for them who need a lamp, a bed for them who need a bed, a slave for all beings who need a slave.[1]

This *Bodhisattva* principle of vicarious living is central to *Mahayana* Buddhism. Each person should strive for Buddha-

[1] *The Path of Light*, Rendered for the First Time into English from the *Bodhicharyavatara* of Santi-deva, by L. D. Barnett (Wisdom of the East series, Murray, London, 1909, 1947), pp. 44-5, 48-9.

realization. The path to that is the path of the *Bodhisattva*. To the question, 'What is the Buddha-mind?' Pure Land Buddhism replies, 'It is no other than the great loving heart.' He who achieves freedom from his blindness does not look down from some monastic retreat upon the unenlightened multitudes. He comes down and mingles with them. Both suffering and goodness are vicarious, for all of creation is bound together. The true saint is he who recognizes this interrelatedness of all life.

> *If I fulfill not my vow by deeds, I shall be false to all beings, and what a fate will be mine! . . . If I labour not this very day, down, down I fall.*[1]

MAHAYANA TEACHING ON THE 'ETERNAL BUDDHA'

Just as the historical Jesus was gradually displaced in Christian teaching by the 'glorified Christ', Gautama Buddha was regarded as being much more than a mere human being. This process—accelerated in early Christianity by the *Fourth Gospel*—was underscored in the *Mahayana* by the *Saddharma Pundarika*. In each case the reverence felt for a master teacher and great spirit led to the articulation of a metaphysical principle. The development of the Christian doctrine of the Trinity over a time span of three centuries was analogous to the process in Buddhism which produced the doctrine of the *Trikaya*, or threefold body.

[1] *Ibid.*, pp. 48-9. Cf. Suzuki, *op. cit.*, p. 57. The *Bodhisattva* concept has been elaborated in many ways in the *Mahayana* schools. My own treatment is considerably condensed. For more elaborate treatments see Har Dayal, *The Bodhisattva Doctrine in Buddhist Sanskrit Literature* (Kegan Paul, Trench, Trübner & Co., London, 1932); B. L. Suzuki, *Impressions of Mahayana Buddhism* (Luzac, London, 1940).

The Christian doctrine of the Trinity and the *Mahayana* doctrine of the *Trikaya* arose among people inclined in a speculative or imaginative direction. Each represented an attempt to interpret subtle areas of human experience, and each interpretation was to prove difficult of comprehension by the common man. Only advanced students of Buddhism go very far into the doctrine of the *Trikaya*, just as the average lay Christian is not expected to understand the Greek doctrine of the Trinity. (The Roman Catholic Church—speaking for the practical Latin temperament—labelled the latter doctrine a 'Mystery' and taught that one could accept it without understanding it.) Since the *Trikaya* doctrine is so important in *Mahayana* Buddhism, a brief word of interpretation is called for even though the temptation may be to follow the path marked out by Rome.

With Gautama, enlightenment was an immediately experienced reality, something which he 'knew' intuitively. *Mahayana* Buddhism sought to give this a metaphysical base in the concept of the *Dharmakaya* (Body of the *Dharma*, or Law). The *Dharmakaya* is the unconditioned spiritual reality, the *essence* of enlightenment and compassion. In Western terms, it might be called the Absolute. More simply, it could be termed Reality—that which must be realized by every being for himself.[1]

The *Sambhogakaya* (Body of Bliss) is the Buddha ideal, or the personification of wisdom. It is the Absolute taking on individuation and working through a Buddha. The *Sambhogakaya* is the 'eternal Buddha' as distinct from the historical Buddha, however. It has been compared to the 'glorified

[1] Detailed explanations differ among *Mahayana* schools. Cf. Suzuki, *Mahayana Buddhism, A Brief Outline*, pp. 42-3.

Christ', but Suzuki compares it to the personal God-concept of Christianity.[1]

The *Nirmanakaya* (Body of Transformation) is the embodied Buddha, the historical Gautama. It partakes of all the characteristics of ordinary flesh, including mortality: hence the name. Every Buddha who appears on earth partakes of the nature of all three *kaya*, yet the Buddha is not three, but One. The *Trikaya* are but aspects of the one Reality.

The *Mahayana* idea that there are many Buddhas who appear on earth to help in the redemption of mankind parallels the teaching of the *Bhagavad Gita*. In the language of the *Gita*, Krishna says, 'For the protection of the good, for the destruction of the wicked and for the establishment of righteousness, I come into being from age to age.' In the Buddhist *Anguttara Nikaya* is to be found the same essential teaching: 'The exalted one appears in the world for salvation to many people, for joy to many people, out of compassion for the world, as a blessing, a salvation, the joy of gods and men.' [2] Both traditions affirm that at the heart of reality there is an outgoing goodness.

NIRVANA IN MAHAYANA BUDDHISM

Nirvana has often been interpreted by Western students of Buddhism as meaning the obliteration of the finite in the infinite. That this is a distortion of the early Buddhist teaching has been indicated in an earlier chapter. It is also to miss the fundamental teaching of the *Mahayana*. According

[1] *Ibid.*, p. 41. Cf. W. M. McGovern, *An Introduction to Mahayana Buddhism* (Kegan Paul, Trench, Trübner & Co., London, 1922), pp. 77 ff.

[2] Cf. *Bhagavad Gita* IV.8 and *Saddharma Pundarika*, ch. 15.

to *Mahayana*, life (or the realm of *samsara*) and *Nirvana* are really identical. In principle, man always is and always has been in *Nirvana*. As the *Awakening of Faith* states it, 'All things from their beginnings are in their nature *Nirvana* itself.' [1]

This doctrine of the identity of *samsara* and *Nirvana*, of the finite and the infinite, appears quite paradoxical to those accustomed to Western modes of thinking, or to the *Hinayana* frame of reference. Yet the doctrine is not as opaque as sometimes made out. Both Alan Watts and Marco Pallis havc made definite contributions in the direction of clarifying the doctrine for serious students.

With respect to the comprehension of Reality, three levels are broadly distinguishable. First, life may be regarded from the point of view of the ordinary man—the point of view of *avidya* or unawareness. To this person life will present itself as a multiplicity with polarity, competitiveness, separateness predominating. The common man is interested in his 'feelings', he takes appearances as though they were the whole story; hence he tends to be a romanticist or sentimentalist.

There is a second point of view which occurs when there is a genuine awakening to the fallacy of regarding the appearances as real. One sees the world as 'illusory'—which does not mean unreal, but that the world 'plays' with our mind and our senses, as it were. He who comes to see the world from this perspective seeks to flee the 'Round of Existence' in order to achieve *Nirvana*. His life is still motivated in terms of polarity or the opposition of two forces. His path is essenti-

[1] A *Mahayana* book frequently attributed to Asvaghosha, who is supposed to have lived around the second century A.D.

ally negative. Those in this state, according to the *Mahayana*, become *Pratyeka Buddhas* (private Buddhas), a term applied by the Mahayanists to the adherents of the *Hinayana* school. For them *Nirvana* remains the *Non-Round*, and the Round is *Non-Nirvana*. The withdrawal of attention from the world (initially necessary if one is to achieve any degree of enlightenment) tends to become a final term. As Pallis comments, when the withdrawal of attention is taken as final, it 'can land one in an intellectual blind alley, bringing about a kind of lofty self-imprisonment, a withdrawal into a blissful supra-consciousness which yet implies privation of the one essential thing, since it stops short of the supreme non-duality'.

The third point of view is that of the *Bodhisattva*. The Round of Existence and *Nirvana* are seen to be identical. One does not have to try the impossible task of getting 'out' of the finite into the infinite, for the infinite is *qualitative* and the finite is *quantitative*. 'A realization of eternity does not involve any leaving of the finite *behind*, because from the eternal standpoint all time is present.' *Nirvana* thus does not mean 'nothingness', but devoid of limiting conditions.[1]

The *Lankavatara Sutra*, one of the important scriptures of *Mahayana*, states the third viewpoint very concisely. 'Those who, afraid of the sufferings arising from the discriminations of birth-and-death (*samsara*), seek for *Nirvana*, do not know that birth-and-death and *Nirvana* are not to be separated from one another; and, seeing that all things subject to dis-

[1] Cf. Alan W. Watts, *The Supreme Identity*, ch. 1, 'The Infinite and the Finite'; M. Pallis, *Peaks and Lamas*, ch. 22, 'The Presiding Idea' (second ed.), especially pp. 305 ff; J. Takakusu, *Essentials of Buddhist Philosophy*, p. 47.

crimination have no (absolute) reality, (they) imagine that *Nirvana* consists in the future annihilation of the senses and their fields.' [1] He who escapes from the dual horns of this dilemma has achieved the supreme realization called the *Prajna Paramita* (Wisdom Transcendent). The *Bodhisattva* has effectively realized it as indicated by his capacity to work actively for the salvation of others in self-less way.

To what extent the articulation of this doctrine in *Mahayana* Buddhism can be traced to the profoundly 'practical' side of the Chinese temperament, and how much to the unfolding of Gautama's own teachings, is not a question that needs to detain us.[2] The intuitive element in the final realization is stressed by all the principal writings such as the *Awakening of Faith*, the *Diamond Sutra* and the *Lankavatara Sutra*. The Buddha, we are told, 'only provisionally makes use of words and definitions to lead all beings, while his real object is to make them abandon symbolism and enter directly into the real Reality'. 'The differentiations of words are but false notions with no basis in reality. . . . But we use words to get free from words until we reach the pure wordless Essence.' [3] Enlightenment comes not by fixed teachings but by an intuitive process that is spontaneous and natural. The Buddha did not lay down a system of teaching, for '"a system of teaching" has no meaning, as Truth cannot be cut up into pieces and arranged into a system'. Whoever uses such a phrase in referring to the teachings of the Buddha is using only a figure of speech.

[1] Watts, *The Supreme Identity*, p. 71.

[2] Cf. Havens, *op. cit.*, p. 30.

[3] *Awakening of Faith*, p. 112. Cf. translation by Wai-tao in Dwight Goddard, *A Buddhist Bible* (second ed., Thetford, Vt., 1938), p. 363.

All conceptions are arbitrary, whether they be about one's own selfhood, other selves, or a universal Self. These should all be discarded as well as 'all ideas about such conceptions and all ideas about the non-existence of such conceptions'. The teacher uses conceptions and ideas in his instruction, but the student must remember that he uses them 'in the resemblance of a raft that is of use only to cross a river'.[1] The validity of things is independent of the validity of words. 'Disciples should be on their guard against the seductions of words and sentences and their illusive meanings, for by them the ignorant and the dull-witted become entangled and helpless as an elephant floundering about in the deep mud.' 'Highest Reality is an exalted state of bliss, it is not a state of word-discrimination and it cannot be entered into by mere statements concerning it.' Whoever teaches a doctrine that is dependent upon letters and words is a mere prattler.[2]

This intuitive realization of *Nirvana* is open to everyone, according to the *Mahayana*. For every man's mind is a mirror of Reality. This latter teaching grew out of the doctrine of the *Alaya-vijnana*—the 'repository consciousness' or the Cosmic Mind from which flow all other forms of consciousness or awareness.[3] To the extent that each person

[1] *The Diamond Sutra* (translated by Wai-tao in Goddard, *op. cit.*, pp. 102, 104, 106).

[2] *Lankavatara Sutra* (translated by Suzuki and Goddard, in Goddard, *op. cit.*, pp. 286, 287, 311).

[3] The concept seems to have had its source as a term in individual psychology, but was given an over-individual or cosmic significance later. Hence Coomaraswamy renders it as 'Cosmic Mind or Reason'. For a brief history of the development of this doctrine, see J. B. Pratt's *Pilgrimage of Buddhism*, pp. 244 ff.

wipes the mirror of his mind clean from stains, he becomes a mirror of Reality, of Buddhahood, of 'pure awareness'. Words, symbols, creeds—all are transcended when one immediately experiences the core of Reality. This development reaches its classical expression in the philosophy of the Zen School (known in China as Ch'an Buddhism).

ZEN BUDDHISM

'Zen never explains; it only gives hints. . . . Trying to explain Zen is like trying to catch wind in a box; the moment you shut the lid it ceases to be wind and in time becomes stagnant air.' This reminder of Alan Watts is a good preface to any attempt to interpret Zen to the West.[1]

For Zen, experience and life are primary. Theories, ritual, concepts are all secondary. Philosophical study as well as ritual can lead one into a jungle from which he cannot extricate himself. Ideas, books, words or forms can only be 'a finger pointing at the moon'. Most people tend to look at the finger instead of the moon. The Zen student must find the moon for himself—the experience of illumination.

Many tools have been devised to help the student achieve this inner realization. Breath control is advised as well as thought control. A more subtle method is that of 'problem solving'. The student is given a problem or *koan* such as: What is the sound of one hand? The *koan* is not to be solved logically. Concentration on the *koan* is to help one sever the ties that bind him to stereotyped responses to life, and thus lead one on to an intuitive awareness of the meaning of living.

[1] Alan W. Watts, *Meaning of Happiness* (Harper, N.Y., 1940), p. 167.

Another type of method in Zen instruction is that of giving an irrelevant reply to a learner's question. The shock method is also used. The teacher may hit the student on the head with his fist, slam a door on his foot, or violently twist his nose. In many such cases the student has been precipitated into a sudden awareness or illumination.

While this experience is sometimes known as Buddha-realization, no student is encouraged to cling to Buddha. 'Cleanse your mouth from the word "Buddha"' is good Zen teaching. No student is a follower of Buddha; he is rather a co-explorer. The basic idea is that *Nirvana*, or self-realization, must be found in the immediate experience of life. One does not seek union with some 'Other'—whether teacher, incarnation or God. He simply seeks to be himself in the most fundamental sense. 'There is nothing infinite apart from things; if you seek something transcendental, that will cut you off from this world of relativity, which is the same thing as the annihilation of yourself.' [1]

A Chinese scholar, Kwaku-An, sought to sum up the meaning of Zen in the twelfth century A.D. by compiling ten poems, traditionally titled *The Ten Oxherding Pictures*. He commented on each verse and made a separate painting for each of the poems. The poems represent ten steps in the realization of one's true nature or selfhood. They are oblique and suggestive and may serve as a fitting conclusion to the study of Buddhism.[2]

[1] D. T. Suzuki, *Eastern Buddhist*, vol. 1, p. 25.

[2] I am indebted to two translations: Nyogen Senzaki and Saladin Reps, *Ten Bulls* (Los Angeles, 1935); and D. T. Suzuki, *The Ten Oxherding Pictures* (Sekai Seiten Kanko Kyokai, Kyoto, 1948).

I

Searching for the Ox

In the pasture of this world, I endlessly push aside
the tall grasses in search of the Ox.
Following unnamed rivers, lost upon the interpenetrating
paths of distant mountains,
My strength is failing and my vitality exhausted. I
cannot find the Ox.
I only hear the locusts chirring through the forest
at night.

In reality it is not the Ox that is lost, but man. Far from home, the man sees many crossroads, but he is unable to decide which way is the right one. Man is alienated from his true nature; his inmost desires are unfulfilled. All he can hear are the locusts of the forests. 'Desire for gain and fear of loss burn like fire; ideas of right and wrong shoot up like a phalanx.' . . . Then he discovers the footprints.

II

Discovering the Footprints

Along the river-bank, under the trees, I discover footprints!
Even under the fragrant grass I see his prints.
Deep in remote mountains they are found.
These traces no more can be hidden than one's nose,
looking heavenward.

Man now gains the first hints of his true nature. He is a long way from his destination, but he has discovered the path. Having begun the search in earnest and harmonized his senses, he perceives the Ox.

III
Perceiving the Ox

I hear the song of the Nightingale.
The sun is warm, the wind is mild, willows are green along the shore,
Here no Ox can hide!
What artist can draw that massive head and those majestic horns!

Man now begins to sense a new unity in his experience. The slightest thing is now seen as not apart from Self, Kwaku-An comments. Everything begins to come into focus.

IV
Catching the Ox

I seize him with a terrific struggle.
His great will and power are inexhaustible.
He charges to the high plateau far above cloud-mists,
Or in an impenetrable ravine he stands.

To master the new insight calls for effort, since the mind is stubborn and unbridled. It has been accustomed to wandering wherever it pleased. The Ox longs for the old sweet-scented fields. It must be brought within bounds.

V
Taming the Ox

The whip and rope are necessary,
Else he might stray off down some dusty road.
Being well trained, he becomes naturally gentle.
Then, unfettered, he obeys his master.

The mind must not be allowed to vacillate. When it wanders, confusion prevails.

VI

Riding the Ox Home

Mounting the Ox, slowly I return homeward.
The voice of my flute intones through the evening.
Measuring with hand-beats the pulsating harmony,
I direct the endless rhythm.
Whoever hears this melody will join me.

The struggle is over. Gain and loss have been assimilated. Man is now self-possessed. His music is spontaneous and harmonious.

VII

The Ox Transcended

Astride the Ox I reach home.
I am serene. The Ox too can rest.
The dawn has come. In blissful repose
Within my thatched dwelling, I have abandoned
the whip and rope.

Duality is now transcended. 'It is like the moon rising out of the clouds.' It is like waking from a dream in which one found himself struggling in the water to keep from drowning. On awaking, one discovers that there was no water. But without the struggle there would have been no waking. In the next stage both Bull and self are transcended.

VIII

Both Ox and Self Transcended

Whip, rope, person and Ox, all merge in No-thing.
This heaven is so vast no message can stain it.
How may a snowflake exist in a raging fire?
Here are the footprints of the Patriarchs.

One no longer seeks even for enlightenment or *Nirvana*. One has returned to the source of his true nature. (The eighth poem is symbolized by an empty circle. A striking parallel to this is Eckhart's idea of 'true spiritual poverty'.[1])

IX

Reaching the Source

Too many steps have been taken in returning to the root and the source.
Better to have been blind and deaf from the beginning!
Dwelling in one's true abode, unconcerned with that without—
The river flows tranquilly on and the flowers are red.

The former roots of action have been destroyed. One now deals with things as they are, without any self-assertion. In place of confused activity, man can now engage in unified activity in the world.

X

In the World

Barefooted and naked of breast I mingle with the people of the world.
My clothes are ragged and dust-laden, and I am ever blissful.
I use no magic to extend my life,
Now, before me, the dead trees become alive.

[1] 'For if one wants to be truly poor, he must be as free from his creature will as when he had not yet been born. For, by the everlasting truth, as long as you will to do God's will, and yearn for eternity and God, you are not really poor; for he is poor who wills nothing, knows nothing, and wants nothing' (Sermon: 'Blessed are the Poor'). R. Blakney, *op. cit.*, p. 228.

As an enlightened person one now lives in the world with a sense of the oneness of all humanity. One no longer searches around for the 'footprints of Patriarchs', for he knows his way without further help from ancient sages. 'I go to the market-place with my wine bottle and return home with my staff. I visit the wineshop and the market and everyone I look upon becomes enlightened.' [1]

. . . . .

This concludes the survey of some of the teachings of Buddhism. In spite of apparent diversity, there is an underlying unity. Only if man comes to see things *as they truly are* can he achieve enlightenment. This intuitive wisdom combined with compassion and true self-less-ness characterize the genuine Buddhist pilgrim. In one way or another, Original Buddhism, Pure Land Buddhism and Zen Buddhism all reveal these elements.

Gautama sought to avoid the jungle of unbridled speculation and the swamp of sentimentalism. Zen Buddhism represents that same spirit. The path so marked out is essentially the razor's edge of the *Upanishadic* philosophers. Each group speaks its own idiom and expresses its own genius. But it is not purely coincidental that in each of these traditions, Hinduism and Buddhism, the dominant concern is that of helping the honest seeker find his true sense of direction.

[1] The wine bottle, or gourd, is the symbol of emptiness (*sunyata*). The staff is the symbol of his functional poverty; he knows that the desire to possess is the curse of finite existence.

CHAPTER NINE

TOWARDS A LARGER FELLOWSHIP

'God never tied man's salvation to any pattern. Whatever possibilities inhere in any pattern of life inhere in all, because God has given it so and denied it to none. One good way does not conflict with another. . . . for not all people may travel the same road.'—Meister Eckhart.

On a shrinking planet, it is important that each man come to a better understanding of his neighbours across the way. The physical fences are down, but too many of the emotional and ideological barriers remain. The preceding chapters have sought to throw light on some aspects of the Hindu and Buddhist metaphysic. It is a teaching of Quakerism that there is something of Truth or God in every man. In Howard Brinton's words, all human beings have had some experience of truth whether they are aware of its nature or not.[1] In a spirit similar to that of liberal Quakerism at its best, let us note in conclusion some of the lessons as well as the problems involved in an appreciative approach to religious traditions other than one's own.

THE RESPONSIBILITY FOR BECOMING AWARE

One of the most important lessons that might be derived from a thoughtful study of Hinduism and Buddhism is the primacy of man's vocation to become *aware* or *awakened*.

[1] Howard Brinton, *Quaker Education in Theory and Practice* (Pendle Hill Pamphlet No. 9, 1949).

Western Christians have frequently tried to sidestep the rigorous task of thinking (especially with reference to first principles) for the easier pastime of sentimentalism in religious living. If one could only 'feel right' with one's God and neighbour, it was too readily assumed that all was well. That a *feeling* of grace or of love is a poor substitute for insights of universal depth is illustrated by a Martin Luther fulminating against 'the thieving rabble of the peasants' or advocating the burning of synagogues. Not all the sermons preached on grace or love can make up for the lack of awareness which leads persons dominated primarily by their feelings into such distorted 'Christian' solutions.

The concern for truth or awareness must be man's first concern. Only as non-awareness is overcome is man freed for compassionate action or intelligent loving. 'Right love' flows from knowledge or a deepened consciousness, and reflects a specific rightness in the nature of things. Love that derives from true insight and right relatedness is qualitatively different from love which flows only from the feelings. The latter is, at best, a healthy by-product of sound psychophysical functioning, and at worst a form of narcissism. The former has distinctly metaphysical dimensions that are drowned out in the turmoil of the love arising from the feelings only.

Marco Pallis has rightly said that Hinduism and Buddhism put much more stress on the duty of combating 'Ignorance' than Christians have. To be sure, Meister Eckhart in speaking of knowledge and love said, 'Knowledge is better than love, but the two together are better than one of them, for knowledge really contains love. Love may be fooled by goodness, depending on it, so that when I love I hang on the gate, but I do not get to God. Thus knowledge is better, for it leads love. Love has to do with desire and purpose, whereas knowledge is no particular thought, but rather it peels off all coverings and is disinterested and runs naked to God, until it touches him and grasps him.' [1] But this is a teaching which has never received too much emphasis in Christian circles.

Obviously the knowledge which is referred to by Eckhart or the Indian sage has little to do with information, beliefs or views. The kind of awareness that is sought is intuitive; it transcends ordinary 'knowing' where the knower stands over against the known. It is a non-dualistic type of knowledge or 'seeing'—a partial clue to which is found in the sense of freedom experienced by the neurotic when he suddenly 'knows' that he has been delivered from his anxiety or his compulsive phobias. To know in this very deep sense, one must be willing to submit to the preparatory discipline. The importance of submission to the disciplines is recognized more fully in the area of the sciences than in the area of religion. Precise preconditions must be met before the scientist can know what he seeks to know. The best scientist is the one most completely alert and most thoroughly disciplined; in short, there must be a synthesis of the live imagination with true *ascesis*, i.e. training. Whenever the house of religion becomes a refuge for marginal men, both imagination and training will be absent.

The West has specialized in pursuing 'utilitarian truths'. It has developed a knack for technological magic and has majored in manipulating the physical environment. Its attitude toward the pursuit of universal Truth, or first principles, has been fluctuating and lackadaisical. This has been re-

[1] *Ibid.*, p. 243. Cf. Marco Pallis, *Peaks and Lamas*, first ed., p. 157.

flected, among other places, in a foreshortened theory of the nature of man. Christian 'otherworldliness' (which has frequently been only a form of postponed hedonism) has tended to assume that man's real destiny lay in the 'after-life'.[1] The emphasis has been neither upon man's knowing himself nor God, but upon 'glorifying' God. This resulted in a very natural stressing of the idea of overwhelming power which found its institutional expressions in the authoritarian church or authoritarian family. Whether one could really 'glorify' God in any meaningful sense before one had come to any understanding of himself, was never properly thought through.

Man is born into a society. His responsibility to society is best met when he seeks to know himself and to discover his vocation. Then he can safely enter the market-place and incidentally assist others in finding themselves. However, one does not blunder into self-knowledge. 'The pursuit of Truth must not be left to chance. No number of charitable actions can be a substitute for that primary need. So-called altruistic actions, if uninformed, are not quite what they purport to be. In so far as they are founded on false premises, they remain ignorant actions and bring forth some of the fruits of ignorance. You cannot gather figs from thistles.' [2] Many a reformer has meddled around in the lives of others when he might fruitfully have been clarifying his own perspective. Where others are awakened to their own potentialities by the work of a reformer, genuine good is accomplished, it is true. One wonders how much more good might have

[1] The very term 'after-life' reveals the primacy of the quantitative yardstick.

[2] Pallis, *op. cit.*, p. 158.

been accomplished if the reformer had opened his own windows first to let the light of knowledge into his own consciousness.

The Christian religion periodically tends to water itself down to a kind of pious sentimentalism. It becomes romanticism in religious garb. Even 'love of God' has been presented so exclusively under sentimental figures that the impression is left that only man's feelings are involved, not his entire mind or being. Rarely has it been stressed with the clarity of a Gandhi that God is *Truth*. To love God unlimitedly means to commit oneself without reservations to the search for Truth. The common temptation is to desire comfort or consolation more than God or Truth. The average Christian's search for an 'insured future' has made the search for Truth a childish search for a God who will see to it that the pain of being born into this kind of world will be rewarded by a heaven of 'an unending stream of pleasures' (to quote one Christian hymn). European man's potentialities for profounder insights have been left slumbering. The perspective of the kindergarten has dominated theology.[1]

THE RELATIVITY OF ALL CONCEPTS

Another lesson that Western man might learn from contact with the East is the relativity of all concepts, including the most 'definitive' concepts of God. Concepts are pointers when used validly. They have a social function in the narrower sense also in that they set up certain limits beyond which the novice in any tribe or culture is not supposed to

[1] Cf. Gerald Heard, 'Vedanta as the Scientific Approach to Religion', in *Vedanta for the West*, edited by Christopher Isherwood (Allen & Unwin, London, 1949).

venture. Every person reaches plateaus periodically in his own experience when he needs to pause briefly to take his bearings. But the primary purpose of the concept is to direct man on down the road yet remaining to be explored.

There is a specific lesson here that Christians need to learn. Time-honoured Christian phrases no longer have the inherent pulling-power for thousands of would-be believers that they once had. One English religionist points out regarding the concept 'Christ', that 'the way forward for faith in the Christendom of this age is to realize that in speaking of Christ men are speaking of God, but that Christ is the historic concept *created by Christendom* in order to realize and speak of God'. Furthermore, 'the reality of God *in our day* lives beyond the concept Christ; the latter can no longer do the work that millions of religious, seeking men demand of it. It no longer sounds the bell of truth in their minds because historic conditions have partly destroyed its validity. That other men do believe, and are forced by experience to believe, that Christ literally is God, is no answer to the disruption of Christendom. They are bound to ask of themselves, at what point does my experience meet the experience —or lack of it—of millions of others, the cast-out mass-men of today?' [1]

A concept is an exploratory tool and is always relative to an experimental situation or a *praxis*. Christians who insist on clinging to their concepts as though absolute display their own spiritual nakedness. Western man is an inveterate idol-worshipper who *thinks* he has moved beyond idolatry. He 'finds' idolatry in the East in one of the more child-like forms in which it is practised; he is unable to see his own more

[1] E. G. Lee, *Mass Man and Religion* (Hutchinson, London, n.d.), p. 146.

complex forms of idolatry. For idolatry can be avoided only when man is aware of what he is doing when he uses symbols, creeds or words in the exploratory process. The most sacred symbols of the past are relative. They are not substitutes for the ongoing wrestling with the problem of meaning in the present. Insights cannot be inherited, they have to be earned. They cannot be caught, they have to be realized.

Christians have suffered from a self-imposed 'rightness and tightness' in this area of concepts. More than religious seekers in the Orient, they have encased themselves in the armour of unexamined assumptions and logic-tight compartments. Canon Streeter has aptly described the predicament of such Christians. 'To live by logic is like playing billiards on board a channel steamer on a choppy day; the better the aim the more certain a miss. The grandest of all follies is to imagine that any words we use or any definition we can frame about God and His dealings with men can have that kind of equivalence to the reality which alone could make them premises for valid logical deduction.' [1] Human life is a complex thing. Theologians with 'views' tend to rush precipitately toward final conclusions.

DANGERS IMPLICIT IN THE CONCEPT 'THE WILL OF GOD'

In the West, where dualism still prevails in orthodox theological thought, 'the will of God' is often taken in an authoritarian rather than exploratory way. This reflects the traditional Western stress on *obedience* or *submission*—a quality emphasizing power more than knowledge, outer authority more than inner light. In the psy-

[1] B. H. Streeter, *The Buddha and the Christ* (Macmillan, N.Y., 1933), p. 138.

chology and metaphysic of the East, the important thing is to achieve *knowledge*: to know the *Atman* is to know *Brahman*. This puts the emphasis—to use Western theological terms—on the *nature of God* rather than the *will of God*. This lessens the tendency to glorify non-rational power at the expense of awareness.

Even regarded from the purely psychological angle, the phrase 'will of God' suffers several drawbacks. For one thing, it is subject to indefinite expansion or contraction at the will of each person, whether the person happens to be emotionally disturbed or spiritually alert. In the history of the Christian Church the 'will of God' has been used profoundly. It has also been debased to justify inhuman courses of action, including brutal warfare against Moslems, Jews and heretics. For a person or institution suffering from delusions of grandeur, the 'will of God' becomes simply a screen or subterfuge. Furthermore, while a mature person may safely pray, 'Not my will but Thine be done', an immature person may gain nothing by submitting his will to that of an 'Other'. An individual may think he has gained a corrected vision by shutting one eye. Actually he has only eliminated his double vision at the loss of perspective.

Every religion includes in its midst many persons aptly styled as 'primitive-minded moderns'. These are the spiritually untutored folk who for a variety of reasons—many beyond their own direct control—have been allowed to remain on childish levels of religious development. For such people emphasis on the 'will of God' perpetuates primitive man's tendency to interpret reality in animistic terms, according to which all objects have 'wills' and are treated as though persons. Personal spirits, both friendly and unfriendly, are found almost everywhere. Anything which arouses a strong emotional response is 'personalized'—misshapen trees, high mountains, thundering cataracts, storms. For people who live in this kind of world, religion becomes a branch of diplomacy.[1] The individual worshipper or the tribe, through the duly ordained 'holy man', tries to cajole, bribe, placate or coerce the various spirits or gods. One inquires into the 'will of God' not in order to know it so much as to use it in the market-place, in the harvest-fields or in battle. Wishes which are thoroughly egocentric are 'sanctified' as prayers, and relics become a kind of talisman for achieving wealth, health or happiness.[2]

Often the professional priesthood is willing to connive with this strange mixture of reverence and superstition, when it is for want of *knowledge* that people perish. Even in our own day, as Canon Streeter has observed, it is held by some that it is better for the common people to believe too much than too little—even at the price of the encouragement of superstition.[3]

As Confucius noted centuries before Jesus, most people sought the 'will of God' (or Heaven) in ways that perpetuated these unfortunate attitudes. Confucius preferred that people explore the whole realm of experience, for, he held, 'Heaven

[1] A. N. Whitehead, *Religion in the Making* (Macmillan, N.Y., 1926), p. 41.

[2] In sixth-century Christianity, 'virtue' (Latin *virtus*) stood for this quasi-magical potency. Devout Christians sought 'virtue' for their own purposes. Gregory, the eminent Bishop of Tours and author of a *History of the Franks*, licked the dust from the rail around St. Martin's tomb in order to be cured of an ailment by the saint's 'virtue'. Gregory of Tours, *History of the Franks* (Trans. by O. M. Dalton; Clarendon Press, Oxford, 1927).

[3] B. H. Streeter, *op. cit.*, p. 79.

does not speak, it *operates*.' The same concern for an 'operational' or exploratory approach seems to underlie the thinking of some contemporary scientists and theologians. If man can be led to explore honestly the *nature of God*, he may be able to determine better 'what the Lord requires of him'.

This shifts the emphasis from a theological category that has too often been an *open sesame* to superstitions and arbitrary conceptions of God to a concern about dependable factors. It is to become aware in modern language of what Jesus sought to make clear when he said that God caused his sun to shine on the unjust as well as the just. Whitehead states the contrast between the two emphases under discussion in the following terms. 'In a communal religion you study the will of God in order that He may preserve you; in a purified religion, rationalized under the influence of the world-concept, you study his goodness in order to be like him. It is the difference between the enemy whom you conciliate and the companion whom you imitate.' He who rises to this outlook of world consciousness thereby transcends the level of communal or tribal awareness. He thus rises above the slippery concept of 'will' to the conception of 'an essential rightness of things'.[1]

To be sure, there are those who simply redefine 'will of God' to mean that which is unchanging, everywhere the same for all races and peoples. This avoids the connotation of arbitrariness, but it is a tacit admission that in God so defined there is a higher category which can be called Law, the Divine Nature or Plato's 'Form of the Good'. This is

[1] A. N. Whitehead, *op. cit.*, p. 41. For another criticism of the idea of personal divine will, see Albert Einstein, *Out of My Later Years* (Phil. Library, N.Y., 1950), pp. 27-9.

another way of going beyond animistic principles of explanation in religion.

BEYOND TOLERANCE TO UNDERSTANDING

Another insight that might be derived incidentally from study of the Eastern tradition is that there are as many ways to the summit of the mountain as there are types of temperament. Hence no religious teacher should ever say, 'Compel them to come in.' Coercion is destructive of the life of the spirit. It focuses upon speedy 'results'. Neither Hindus nor Buddhists are too worried about the time factor. No Inquisition ever made its appearance among them. Spirituality cannot be forced any more than the delicate string of a clavichord can stand undue tension. In place of compulsion there must be impulsion, arising within the person as he becomes aware of his vocation. No man ever is; he is always in process of becoming. In just what sense 'no man is an island' can be determined experientially through the extension of each man's area of awareness.

Tolerance is a negative concept which implies that the diversity of means are as significant as the end sought. What that *one end* is, is something which can be most effectively realized when one is not shadow-boxing with prejudices rooted in fear and ignorance. No healthy child goes through an emotional crisis when he discovers that the world is not flat and that there is no absolute up or down. Similarly, no healthy adult is disturbed by revolutionary changes in religious terminology when events demand them. The past holds man in its embrace even as water holds the swimmer. Man does himself an injustice in trying to hold it. When the human body is functioning well, it does not cling to its past.

The old skin disappears, bones change and the person thinks nothing of it. The fingers of the hand do their intricate manœuvres; millions of years went into the development of that structure. The hand fashioned by a long past does not cling to that past; it does the work of the present. In the genes and chromosomes countless ancestors survive in each man in some sense. Since man's ancestors live on in him, he does not need to concern himself too much about revering them. If the lessons were properly learned and remain in keeping with environmental demands, man remains unaware of those lessons.

The religious teachings of the past should not be ensconced in way-side shrines tempting man to tarry too long. The only place where man can come to himself is in the present. The growing person is dying to himself constantly; so are religious systems that retain any vitality. On the world landscape of religion, many people with differing cultural backgrounds find their places. Each religion wears a garb peculiar to itself. Each expresses some of the values of the past, but no garb is sacred in an absolute sense.

As these religions become better acquainted with the best in each tradition, including their own, a new spirit will replace the older competitiveness. Underlying the richness of diversity will be an ever-widening fellowship of honest men. Differences will not disappear, but they will be seen in a wider perspective. World community will not mean world faith in the sense that one religion will displace all of the others or synthesize them. It will involve, however, world-mindedness and a respect for diversity even while all honest inquirers are seeking to discover the more universal implications of their own starting-points.[1]

[1] Cf. W. E. Hocking, *Living Religions and a World Faith*, chs. 3-4.

Historical near-sightedness is an inheritance from the days of isolated continents and peoples. Present planetary needs demand world community. The unique quality of every land and religion can be respected on a shrinking planet wherever that uniqueness is held in such a way that it imposes no barriers to the widening fellowship that man's nature demands.

World community on a purely quantitative basis is no solution, however. Fellowship is a matter of the spirits of men. The deeper the *quality* of the relatedness, the richer is the experience of community. Man can only build community in the present. He builds community in a profound sense only when his efforts are bent in the direction of extending his area of awareness through total dedication to the knowledge of Truth or God.

True community or fellowship is capable of indefinite enrichment. The followers of the various religious teachers of mankind can create this kind of community to the extent that they *cease being followers and become co-explorers.* Jesus, Gautama, Lao-tse, Socrates and the anonymous *Upanishadic* sages are not really so far apart as their respective followers have made them. Teachings of famous men can at their best be only pointers, like road-signs at important intersections in the highways of life. To cling to a road-sign or to quibble over the meaning of its language is to forget the journey.

Life is a journey which authenticates itself to those who have the confidence to explore. Man's calling is to the open road. An invitation to the realization of Truth is not an invitation to a debating society or to religious competitiveness. It is an invitation to live—and to live more abundantly.

GLOSSARY OF TERMS

This glossary is intended only as a guide for the beginning student. Many terms which occur only once in the book are not included in this listing. Except where otherwise indicated, the words are Sanskrit.

Adharma. In Hinduism, disequilibrium. Its ethical connotation, unrighteousness.

Dharma. In Hinduism, equilibrium, norm or law. Its ethical dimension, righteousness or morality. (In the Pali, *dhamma*. For a Buddhist meaning, see p. 124.)

Anatta (Pali). Non-*Atman* or non-Self. Interpreted in early Buddhism as meaning a denial of an enduring soul or ego.

Anicca (Pali). Impermanence, transience.

Atman. In Hinduism, the absolute unconditioned Spirit, the real Self; also the reflection of the Absolute (*Brahman*) in the individual.

Atman-jnana. Self-knowledge; knowledge of the Real.

Avidya. Ignorance, spiritual blindness, unawareness.

Vidya. Knowledge, awareness (from a root meaning 'to see').

Bhakti-yoga. The pathway of faith or loving devotion.

Bodhisattva. Literally 'wisdom being'; one whose nature consists of insight, dedicated to the salvation of others.

Brahman. The Absolute or Supreme Reality, from a root meaning 'power'. Also applied to the man of power, the priest.

Brahma. The Supreme Reality manifested as personal God so-called, or God as creator.

Isvara. God-as-personal (in the general Christian sense); *Saguna Brahman* (literally 'Brahman-with-attributes').

Brahmanas. Ritual commentaries; one of the main sections of the traditional wisdom (*Veda*).

Brahman-vidya (or *Brahmavidya*). Knowledge of Brahman.

Buddha. An awakened one. Refers to Gautama after he obtained enlightenment, or to others who have reached the point of awakening.

Dharma. See above, *Adharma.*

Duhkha (Pali). Usually translated suffering, imperfection, pain. More exactly, commotion, agitation, or disharmony. Expressed psychologically as dis-ease or suffering.

Gunas. The three 'strands', elements or forces forming the twisted rope of nature. At thc psychological level, the three components of the empirical self.

Guru. Spiritual teacher or guide.

Jiva (or *Jivatma*). Individual ego or 'soul'; the Supreme Reality particularized in the individual.

Karma. Action or work; also action-influence (hence character).

Karma yoga. The way of works. Sometimes interpreted as meaning only ritualistic worship. In the *Gita,* combined explicitly with the idea of humanitarian or disinterested action.

Karuna. Compassion; the outstanding characteristic of the *Bodhisattva* in Mahayana Buddhism.

Maya. The phenomenal world; the world as it appears to the ordinary person who is unaware. See A. K. Coomaraswamy's *On Translation of Maya, Deva, Tapas* (St. Catherine Press Ltd., Bruges, Belgium, reprint, April 1933).

Moksha. Release, freedom from fragmentariness or the realm of flux; liberation.

Neti, neti. 'Not this, not this'; the path of negation to be followed by the one desiring Self-knowledge or knowledge of Brahman.

Nirvana. Literally 'despiration' or 'a blowing out' (as of a flame); extinction. On the ethical level, the dying out of lust, resentment, covetousness. On the psychological level, extinction of individuality.

Parinirvana. Complete *Nirvana*; also simply dissolution.

Samadhi. Superconsciousness; highest state of contemplation; the unitive state.

Samsara. Literally 'stream' or 'confluence'; stream of becoming; eternal recurrence ('transmigration').

Tanha (Pali). Thirst, craving, inordinant desire.

Tapas. Literally 'burning' or 'glow'; hence intension, toil or austerity.

Trikaya. The 'three bodies' or modes of a Buddha; in Mahayana doctrine.

Tripitaka. 'Three baskets' or collections. The Pali Buddhist canon, consisting of *Vinaya*, *Sutta* and *Abhidhamma*.

Upadana. Clinging; associated with *tanha* in Buddhist analysis.

Upaya. Accommodation, convenient means; in Mahayana doctrine.

Vedanta. 'End of the Veda.'

Vidya. See above, *Avidya*.

Yoga. Literally 'to yoke'. Used in two senses: (1) union (of the *Atman* and *Brahman*); (2) the pathway to such union, or the discipline involved.

BIBLIOGRAPHY

For the person who wants to make a more detailed study of the Oriental traditions dealt with in this volume, the following books are suggested.

For the earliest writings of Hinduism and Buddhism, in English translations, the reader is referred to such collections as:

Sacred Books of the East.
Sacred Books of the Buddhists.
Pali Text Society Translation Series.
Harvard Oriental Series.

Many of the first translations made by Western scholars are quite misleading. They should be supplemented, where possible, with the translations of Coomaraswamy, Prabhavananda, Nikhilananda, D. T. Suzuki, Radhakrishnan.

The Upanishads in Translation

Swami Nikhilananda, *The Upanishads* (Harper, N.Y., 1949, vol. 1).

Swami Prabhavananda and F. Manchester, *The Upanishads, Breath of the Eternal* (Vedanta Press, Hollywood, 1947).

R. E. Hume, *The Thirteen Principal Upanishads* (Oxford Univ. Press, 1921).

F. Max Müller, *The Upanishads* (*Sacred Books of the East*, vol. 1, 15, Clarendon Press, Oxford, 1879, 1884).

The Bhagavad Gita in Translation

Some of the earlier translations are those by K. T. Telang (1882), Edwin Arnold (1885), M. M. Chatterji (1887), A. M. Sastri (1901), L. D. Barnett (1905), Sri Aurobindo (1928), W. D. P. Hill (1928), B. G. Tilak (1935), D. S. Sarma (1937).

Of the more recent translations, two include the Sanskrit text in Romanized letters: Franklin Edgerton (1944) and S. Radhakrishnan (1948).

Two other excellent translations are those by Swami Prabhavananda and Christopher Isherwood (1945), and Swami Nikhilananda (1944).

Books on Hinduism or Buddhism

Swami Akhilananda, *Hindu Psychology, Its Meaning for the West* (Kegan Paul, 1946). A popular introduction designed for Western readers and drawing considerably from Western thought to aid the interpretation.

Ananda K. Coomaraswamy, *Am I My Brother's Keeper?* (John Day, N.Y., 1947). A series of essays which make an excellent introduction to the important work done by this eminent scholar.

A New Approach to the Vedas (Luzac, London, 1933). Includes portions of two *Upanishads* and three *Vedic* hymns. An excellent essay in translation and exegesis, not for the beginner.

Buddha and the Gospel of Buddhism (Harrap, London, 1928). A volume to be read with both pleasure and profit by the beginner.

Hinduism and Buddhism (Philosophical Library, N.Y., 1943). A compact, richly annotated interpretation of basic Hinduism and Buddhism, going beyond his earlier work of 1928. Unsurpassed, but not for the layman.

Religious Basis of the Forms of Indian Society (N.Y., 1946).

Paul Deussen, *Philosophy of the Upanishads* (Clark, Edinburgh, 1906, 1919). One of the best of the early studies. Its Western philosophical terminology sometimes misleading.

The System of the Vedanta, According to Badarayana's Brahma-Sutras and Sankara's Commentary Thereon Set Forth as a Compendium of the Dogmatics of Brahmanism from the Standpoint of Sankara (Open Court, Chicago, 1912). Same qualification applies.

Rene Guenon, *East and West* (Luzac, London, 1941). Basic differences between Occidental and Oriental frames of reference. Good as an introduction to Guenon's works.

The Crisis of the Modern World (Luzac, London, 1942).

Introduction to the Study of the Hindu Doctrine (Luzac, London, 1945). Excellent.

Man and His Becoming According to the Vedanta (Luzac, London, 1945). Excellent.

William McGovern, *Introduction to Mahayana Buddhism* (Kegan Paul, London, 1922). General survey of the Mahayana.

Swami Prabhavananda, *Vedic Religion and Philosophy* (Sri Ramakrishna Math, Mylapore, Madras, India, 1943). Excellent introduction for the thoughtful layman.

Marco Pallis, *Peaks and Lamas* (2nd edition, Knopf, N.Y., 1949). Excellent chapters on 'The Presiding Idea' and 'The Round of Existence'. Mahayana Buddhism.

James B. Pratt, *The Pilgrimage of Buddhism* (Macmillan, N.Y., 1928). Covers the entire field of Buddhism. Best one-volume text available in English. Uneven in depth of interpretation; appreciative.

S. Radhakrishnan, *The Philosophy of the Upanishads* (Allen & Unwin, London, 1924). A good secondary study for the mature beginner.

N. Senzaki and S. Reps, *Ten Bulls* (Mentor garten, Los Angeles, 1935).

Beatrice L. Suzuki, *Impressions of Mahayana Buddhism* (Luzac, London, 1940).

Mahayana Buddhism, A Brief Outline (Marlowe, London, 1948). Excellent for beginner.

D. T. Suzuki, *Essays in Zen Buddhism*, 3 vols. (Luzac, London, 1927, 1933; vol. 3, Harper, N.Y., 1949).

Introduction to Zen Buddhism (Philosophical Library, N.Y., 1949). An excellent introduction by the outstanding Zen scholar.

The Lankavatara Sutra (London, 1932). Translation of one of the most important sources of Mahayana Buddhism. For the advanced student.

Studies in the Lankavatara Sutra (Routledge, London, 1930).

The Zen Doctrine of No-Mind (Rider, London, 1949).

J. Takakusu, *The Essentials of Buddhist Philosophy* (Univ. of Hawaii, Honolulu, 1949). First three chapters more general; the remainder is a detailed study of different Mahayana schools.

A. W. Watts, *The Spirit of Zen* (Murray, London, 1948).

Zen (Stanford, Palo Alto, 1948).

The Supreme Identity (Pantheon, N.Y., 1950). An excellent essay on Oriental metaphysic and the Christian religion.

H. Zimmer, *Myths and Symbols in Indian Art and Civilization* (Pantheon, N.Y., 1946).

INDEX

(See Glossary of Terms also)